POLITICAL PHILOSOPHY OF AMBEDKAR

POLITICAL PHILOSOPHY OF AMBEDKAR

An Inquiry into the Theoretical Foundations of the Dalit Movement

P. Kesava Kumar

KALPAZ

First Published 2014

Published by

Kalpaz Publications
C-30, Satyawati Nagar,
Delhi - 110052
E-mail: kalpaz@hotmail.com Ph.: 9212142040

Laser Typesetting : Deepak Shukla, Delhi
Printed at : Chawala Offset Printers, Delhi

Cataloging in Publication Data--DK
Courtesy: D.K. Agencies (P) Ltd. <docinfo@dkagencies.com>

Kēśava Kumār, Pi
Political philosophy of Ambedkar : an inquiry into the theoretical foundations of the dalit movement / P. Kesava Kumar.
p. cm.
Includes bibliographical references (p.) and index.
ISBN 9788178359847

1. Ambedkar, B. R. (Bhimrao Ramji), 1891-1956--Political and social views. 2. Dalits--Political activity--India. I. Title.

DDC 305.56880954 23

Dedication

For my mother

Late P. Nagendramma

Contents

Foreword

Political Philosophy of Ambedkar: An Inquiry into the Theoretical Foundations of the Dalit Movement is a work of distinctive nature which is constituted by two apparently related areas of political philosophy of Ambedkar and theory of Dalit movement and yet so different as emerging theoretical concerns and political practices. Dalit movement is an emerging concern while its theory is not very frequently discussed. Philosophy of Ambedkar has recently attracted attention of scholars, but it has not yet developed clear contours. Thus the work ventures into terrains rarely explored. The task becomes daunting when one attempts to deepen understanding borrowing from different fields and simultaneously creating a new field. The work under discussion is not merely trying to be an academic exercise but, more significantly driven by political logic of emancipation of Dalits. Hence, the work sets for itself multiple tasks which require borrowing from various fields. Analysing Ambedkar's thought requires skills of analytical philosophy. Dalit movement has been approached from the view point of sociology of politics while other fields like literature and films have been interrogated using critical tools from Cultural studies. Dr. Kesav Kumar's choice of themes in enquiring into Dalit Movement like literature, films, struggles over democratisation of university, atrocities against Dalits etc., itself shows the influence of new fields, as a consequence sheds light on new aspects. Here I would attempt to paint the context of the work and the author and focus on determinations shaping the work.

Dr. Kesav's academic work is reflective of his political concerns. It cannot be separated from the context of his political engagement which he himself described as it had begun during anti-Mandal agitation. Though the event anti-Mandal agitation has been key in crystalisation of a certain type of democratic politics of Dalits, there had been unreflective institutions shaping ones social and political orientation with in Telugu culture. Literature is one such institution which has helped one to grow beyond one's life contexts and develop public notions of love of one's country and people. Telugu literature has been the formative context of many public intellectuals. Kesav had been influenced by Telugu literature and a creative writer by himself.

Dalit movement had come into existence during anti-Mandal agitation. It led to emergence of new solidarities based on caste in the public space particularly in colleges and universities. It torn apart the image of public institutions as casteless neutral spaces. Mobilisations were led by left wing radical activists at that point of time due to absence of traditions of public activism of autonomous nature among Dalits. Left wing activism is distinct from Dalit activism. Left wing activists' understanding of the world is mediated by books. They view world as an objective entity whose nature needs to be grasped in order to change it. Left wing activism requires capacities for abstract imagination. Capacities for abstraction take one to the level of leading public mobilisations as they can know better the dynamics of it. This conception of activism did continue even after the emergence of Dalit movement and women's movement which had extensive influence in post 90's in Andhra Pradesh. Dalit Mobilisations and women Mobilisations radically reinvented conception of public activism, but a significant stream among them continued to go by left notions of public activism. This conception continued even among a section of Dalit activists and women activists. Right understanding comes from right knowledge and right knowledge, Kesav thinks, is available in the ideas of Ambedkar.

Dalit activism does not imagine an activist to be a bearer of objective knowledge. An activist grows out of one's involvement in different activities of life. He leads in work and other contexts of public and private interaction. It requires an intense grasp of one's practical activity. Without this, one cannot lead at various levels and mobilise people. For them, Ambedkar has been of immense significance as a symbol. Kesav's attempt has been to explore the significance of Ambedkar as a symbol and as a thinker and to particularly bring our attention to unrealised democratic potential of ideas and practice of Ambedkar.

Thinking of intellectual influences, it is worthy to begin metaphorically with the title of his first chapter: Ambedkar: Philosopher of Our Times. The phrase "Our Times" is enormously revealing. For him, it represents time of uncertainty of ideals and hence, requiring complex response. It was an uncertainty of one's belief in possibility of revolutionary change. And, it was also time of emergence of Dalit movement ad women's movement which changed the public perception of ongoing happenings. Revolutionary subject has been discredited and he has been analysed to show that he is having biases of upper caste male. New issues came into the public domain like atrocities against

Dalits, harassment against women in places of work etc which could not be addressed by traditional Marxian analysis. This is what our times imply. He believes Ambedkar is relevant for such times. The idea of philosopher is also differently used. Philosopher need not necessarily be evaluated by depth and rigour of academic grasp of the issue. Philosopher is one whose ideas act as catalyst for emancipation of the oppressed. Ambedkar is a philosopher of this kind having relevance for our times. The second part of the work is about context while the first part represents intellectual response to that context.

His immediate intellectual context has been changes in the institution of Literature. It has been criticised that revolutionary literature of the times has become immobilised because it has lost touch with social churning and had remained upper caste in nature in the sense that the use of poetic language is of such nature. It has been iterated that Dalit literature should be authored by Dalits themselves as it can only authentically represent their experience. Marxism has been replaced by Ambedkarism as a guiding philosophy for liberation of Dalits and Bahujans in literature. It was one of the determining influences in Andhra Pradesh.

Emergence of Cultural studies also changed the nature of academic endeavour. Methodologically, the field has shifted from analysis of material forces to culture and culture as constituting power relations. It led to critically analysing hidden forms of domination against women, Dalits and sexually marginalised in new spaces. These new spaces are films, literature, and university etc., supposedly modern spaces with universal access. Cultural studies unpacked ideological hegemony of universal spaces and laid bare the inability of disciplines to uncover hidden biases of such universal spaces. This forms the intellectual context of the author which constituted the work.

The work consists of two parts. The second part provides us with an understanding of the present. It is a sort of contemporary archive. It covers variety of themes like Dalit movement, literature, films, university, inter dynamics of caste and gender, etc., from the perspective of Dalit movement. The first part is a sort of wrestling from the context to understand the nature of various social and political institutions and its implications to the practice of Dalit movement drawing from within Ambedkar's thought.

In the second part, he has written on modernity and Dalits. He argues that modernity has been monopolised by Brahmins. Brahmins themselves adapted scientific epistemologies and assumed significant positions in scientific establishment. As they practiced modernity in academic pursuits, social modernity remained elusive. It did not reach Dalits and they were excluded from accessing benefits of modernity. He points to the fact of pretentious nature of universal access of modern institutions. Modern institutions apparently seem to be accessible to everyone. But the access has been restricted by certain type of codification of the normal. Presence of some appears to be normal while exclusion of Dalits also understood as normal. Any attempt to question this is seen as castiest. Thus, he criticises caste bias inherent in modern institutions.

Dr. Kesav incisively analyses various aspects of condition of Dalits with new tools. He brings our attention to caste atrocities arising as a consequence of caste based discrimination in Andhra Pradesh. It sharply focuses on new aspirations of Dalits to attain share in political power and BSP as a realisation of such an aspiration. Issues of internal democratisation within Dalits also have been highlighted. He analysed institutions like literature and films with new perspectives drawn from cultural studies. He analyses film as a text which is made to manage conflicting social desires with in a coherent narrative of the film. In film viewing it enabled agency to marginalised castes by mobilising desire into a socially meaningful coherent unity. He also referred to emergence of Dalit literature as a reflection of emergence of autonomous Dalit movement. This context made it necessary to go to Ambedkar's ideas to reinterpret them to understand new context of Our Times and formulate relevant ideals for emancipation of Dalits.

He refers to interpretation of key ideals available in Ambedkar's thought. Democracy must be in the realm of social and economic, but political democracy alone cannot bring about necessary changes. Democracy in social sphere is of essential significance to the transformation of condition of Dalits. Social reform must precede political reform. Reforming religion is key to reconstruction of the social. Ambedkar denounces inegalitarian Hindu religion and advocates more humane and compassionate religion, i.e., Buddhism. Caste is the key social institution which destroys the spirit necessary for humane and just society. It can be built only by destroying caste. Thus, it has been attempted in the work to construct alternative ideals for Dalit movement.

P. Kanaka Rao
Faculty in Political Science
Assam University
Silchar, Assam

Preface

I come from a Dalit family that lives in a village called Amruthalur located in Guntur district of the Coastal Andhra. I was an innocent lad from the village when I entered University of Hyderabad Campus for my post-graduation. Here various instances and experiences sensitized me better to know myself and the context in which I live. The first major incident which drew my attention was the "Mandal Commission Agitation" of the 1990s. The country was going through a new phase of social change which brought to the surface the tensions involved in addressing the caste question. On the issue of reservations I witnessed that the whole country was polarized into pro-Mandal and anti-Mandal groups. Additionally, the Tsundur massacre of 1991 and autonomous dalit struggles against caste violence in Andhra Pradesh changed the political discourse in a significant way. In these circumstances our University became an active platform for addressing the problem of caste and the future of these struggles centered on this. I also involved myself in the post-Mandal struggles of the University students, and the challenges of these struggles related to the caste question provoked me providing me insights to take up this present study. I am thankful to students' who participated, rebelled and sacrificed for the good of the society.

The 1990's was politically a turbulent period in Andhra Pradesh which influenced me a lot. The Maoist revolutionary struggles, womens' struggles, Dalit struggles, and Dandora struggles were active and each of them was also politically and philosophically negotiating with the other. Directly or indirectly I have associated myself with the changing political and literary discourse of time. However, I have looked at all these struggles from my own dalit subjective position. In this social context, I have gone through the writings of Dr. B.R. Ambedkar which proved a liberating force of oppressed masses. At the same time I have realized that the philosophy of Ambedkar needs to be creatively interpreted rather than devotionally followed. In this journey, I have tried to engage myself with the writings of radical Ambedkar who questioned the dominance and struggled uncompromisingly against the centers of power and knowledge.

I'm greatly indebted to the Indian Council of Philosophical Research (ICPR) for providing me an opportunity to work on this project. Especially I am thankful to Dr. Mercy Helen for constantly persuading me to complete this work.

I am thankful to my beloved friend Kanaka Rao, faculty of Assam University who has been participating with me in the many struggles of the University of Hyderabad and constantly engaging me in the intellectual debates. I thank Dr. Bindu K.C. for giving me her precious time in proof reading the draft and for valuable suggestions to improve it.

I thank all my teachers of Department of Philosophy, University of Hyderabad and my colleagues at Pondicherry University. I thank my friends – Dr. Aneel Babu, Dr. R. Vijay, Dr. J. Ravindranath, Dr. G Lakshmi Prasad, Dr. R. Seshagiri Rao, G Dharma Rao, B. Satyanarayana, Dr. Nagaraju, Mohammad Abbas, Dr. Sridhar, Dr. Darla Venkateswara Rao, Dr. Sudarshan, Dr. Ravindra Babu, Dr. G Narsaiah, Dr. S. Sudhakar, Kathi Kalyan, Kiran Kumar, Vijaya Bhaskar – at the University of Hyderabad for refreshing my memories, and of course for their company and hospitality. I thank my well wishers and Dalit Scholars- Dr. K.Y. Ratnam, Dr. P. Tirumal, Dr. B. Chandrasekhar Rao of University of Hyderabad, Dr. B. Easwar Rao of Assam University, Dr. Y. Srinivasa Rao of Bharatidasan University, Dr. Y. Cinnna Rao of JNU, Dr. N. Sukumar of Delhi University, Dalit poet Kalekuri Prasad and Palnati Sreeramulu of Bahujana Keratalu. I thank my friend late Dr. S. Amanualla for his emotional support at Pondicherry University.

I thank dalit scholar and Ex-M.L.A. of Viduthalai Chiruthaigal Katchi of Tamil Nadu, D. Ravi Kumar (Pondicherry) for sharing his views on dalit politics.

I am genuinely indebted to my mother late Nagendramma who has struggled hard to help me reach this level. I'm equally thankful to my wife Dr. Rajeswari and my beloved daughters Akshara and Asmitha for making me happy.

P. Kesava Kumar

1

Ambedkar: Philosopher of Our Times

There are several attempts to understand Ambedkar and his philosophy. Confusion prevails among scholars due to the existence of diverse, and sometimes, contradictory theoretical assessment of Ambedkar. The social context of the scholars and their subjective positions play major role in the assessment of the thinker and very often the opinions of scholars evoke extreme reactions which either elevate, or demean Ambedkar. Though he had a great influence on Indian politics from the nationalist movement onwards, till eighties, there has been not much academic debate on Ambedkar. The communities of knowledge and centres of power either ignored, or deliberately marginalised him as a thinker and social scientist. Very interestingly, the masses communities of underprivileged of Indian society bring him into the forefront. It is not exaggeration to say that there is no major village in the country without the statue of Ambedkar. He is the most celebrated symbol of the contemporary times. Due to the 'masses'/'Dalit communities' symbolic association with Ambedkar, political parties and academics ranging from conservatives to radicals, are forced to look at Ambedkar. The celebration of Ambedkar has the undercurrent of failure of Indian democratic State to reach the majority of this nation, and the assertion of these ignored communities. In other words, Ambedkar's philosophy is a search towards the theories of social reconstruction of Indian society.

Ambedkar is nowhere mentioned in the contemporary *Indian philosophy* and the philosophical discourses of India. This exclusion of Ambedkar has to be understood with the implicit politics of the writers on *Indian philosophy*. One may find problems with the basic assumptions of writers on *Indian philosophy*, as they never overcome the certain dogmas and myths about Indian philosophy. As *S.N. Dasgupta* explains, many of these writers/philosophers had affinity with some dogmas in developing *Indian philosophy* (e.g., the doctrine of rebirth, doctrine of *moksha* and theory of *karma).* This made them subservient to ethics and religion in writing *Indian philosophy.* For instance, belief in theory of *karma* justifies that the social inequalities of present life are determined by the unknown activities of past life. Likewise, many of the writers on *Indian philosophy* are carried by these dogmas, without having a critical look at them. Whereas, *Dasgupta* argues against these kind of dogmas carried by the Indian philosophers. He felt that the immediate imperative of Indian philosophy is to *rejuvenate* and revitalise itself by critical reformation of the fundamental postulates that have so long been guiding its destiny.[1]

In the same manner, *Dayakrishna* critically considers the myths about Indian philosophy that are influencing the writers in the conception and presentation of *Indian philosophy* (i.e., *Indian philosophy* is exclusively spirituals, the acceptance of authority of veda, and development and classification of Indian philosophical schools). In this context he explains that most of the presentations of Indian philosophy are nonhistorical in nature. History is always the story of change, development, differentiation, or innovation. But most of the writers/ philosophers on Indian philosophy are immune to change. He considers that the dead and mummified picture of Indian philosophy will be alive only when it is seen to be a living stream of thinkers who have grappled with difficult problems that are philosophically, as alive today as they were in the ancient past. Indian philosophy will become contemporarily relevant only when it is conceived as philosophy proper. For him philosophy is a living tradition.[2] These debates inform the *ahistorical* nature of Indian philosophy and its social irrelevance.

Philosophy is a social expression. It is always conditioned by the social life. Philosophers have to reflect on the social and cultural practices in which they lived. In India, caste is the fundamental social reality that shapes and influences everyday life. It is determining force in one's perception of the world. As *Pratima Bowes* rightly observed,".... The philosophers in India failed in their task in as much as they did nothing towards developing political, social, or moral philosophy in India. One reason for this non-development may be that philosophical thought was a monopoly of the Brahmin caste, whose privileges would have been under attack if questions were to be asked about the social system"[3].

The intellectuals of the Indian renaissance to resist the hegemony of the *colonialism* interpreted the past for their immediate demands. The nationalist intellectuals happen to be elites of the Brahminical class and reflected from their own social imagination in constructing the Indian philosophy. 'In their search for internal principle of unity to the past, religion was given a foundational position by both orthodox and reformist Brahmin intellectuals'.[4] This can be seen in torch bearers of modern India like *Rajaramohun Roy*, *Dayananda Saraswati*, *Sri Aurobindo*, *Tagore*, *Vivekananda*, *Tilak*, *Gandhi*, *Radhakrishnan* etc.[5] The Hindu nationalists started the tradition of dressing up the spirit centred metaphysics of orthodox *Hinduism* in modern scientific clothes.[6] The modern Hindu intellectuals are very much aware of the social contradictions of the Indian society, but they never attempted seriously to change the society. They responded to the situation indirectly in such a way that it does not effect their socially privileged position. To conceal the contradictions of the Indian society, the renaissance and nationalist intellectuals were clever enough to invent a new language that works well.[7]

Parallel to this dominant Brahminical philosophical tradition, there exists a powerful philosophical stream of the lower castes which is ignored by these brahminical elites. Their knowledge systems and life styles are not considered as the regimes of truth. In fact, they developed their philosophy from the condemned life styles and socio-cultural practices. It is not an exaggeration to say that philosophers of lower castes of India made an attempt to democratise the philosophical traditions of India. In the late medieval period there were many philosophers/yogis from the artisan communities who exposed the hollowness of the philosophies of Brahminical Hinduism by using the same philosophical principles proposed by the philosophers of caste Hindus. In contemporary times, Ambedkar is one such a philosopher. His intervention in Indian philosophy is crucial and significant in many ways. He represents living philosophical tradition. His approach to

Indian philosophy is rational and practical rather speculative and dogmatic. He evaluates the Indian philosophy from historical perspective. His philosophy is 'this worldy', 'realistic' and 'man-centred' rather 'otherworldly', 'transcendent', 'idealistic', and 'god centred'. His philosophy enriched with social and cultural practices of Indian society. He philosophised the social experiences in order to change the world of oppression and humiliation. He proves that philosophy emerges from the social struggles but not in isolation.

About Ambedkar there are diverse opinions. Upper caste Nationalists has tried to brand him as a 'British agent'. For instance, *Arun Shourie*, the Hindu nationalist, the "intellectual hero" of the upper castes at the time of the anti-Mandal agitation and the Minister for Disinvestment in one of the BJP-led government, puts all his efforts to depict him as an anti-national collaborator with British imperialism in his book *Worshipping false Gods, Ambedkar and the Facts which have been Erased (1997).*[8] He charged that in the 1940s, Ambedkar never took part in any freedom movement. Instead, he was collaborating with the British. The motive of the Brahminical Hindu nationalists is quite clear. They want to prove that Ambedkar does not have any political credentials to be worshipped as a god of 'social justice'. This attitude has to be understood in the wake of a strong *Dalit movement* and their confrontation with Hindu nationalism and caste hegemony. Ambedkar is the symbol and source of philosophy for Dalits in pursuit of their struggles. In response to this, the upper caste Hindu nationalist thinker *Arun Shourie*, through his writings, consciously tried to neutralise the influence of Ambedkar in post-independent Indian politics in general and among Dalit masses in particular.

Naxalite parties like CPI (ML) (Peoples War Group) place him as a liberal bourgeoisie democrat. (At present it is known as CPI (Maoist) party).[9] Ranganayakamma, identified as a Marxian writer, argues in her book that neither Ambedkarism, Buddhism has the real potential to liberate Dalits. Only *Marxism* has the capacity to liberate them totally.[10] Some would like to see him as a conservative, because of his leanings towards religion, *Buddhism*. However, there is an immediate emotional response to all the above remarks from the conscious Dalit scholars and masses.

On the other side, Dalit parties like *Bahujan Samaj Party*, or some Dalit scholars, argue that Ambedkar is the only radical thinker of the nation. For liberation of the Dalit masses, Ambedkar is the only solution. They took him to the level of a god. In this regard, Dalit scholar *Anand Teltumbde* comments, 'in making Ambedkar as a demigod, we are missing his essential message.'[11] One may encounter similar kind of problems in theorising Ambedkar's philosophy.

It is clear that everyone has his/her intentions and motives in attributing particular political positions to Ambedkar. Along with the Brahminical Hindu writers, the nationalist Congress also calls him a British agent. With this, it is easy for them to exclude him from the pride of the nationalist movement. Naxalite parties call him a liberal democrat. Their intention is to show that he is not a radical thinker. As said earlier, they believe that the liberation of Dalits is only possible through a sound philosophy like Marxism-Leninism and Maoism.[12] According to them, class politics can accommodate more political space than caste. In this country, through democratic means people could not achieve anything. Only through armed struggle, the Dalit masses can get real political power. The Naxalite parties expect Dalits to be in their fold rather getting attracted towards existing Dalit political parties based on Ambedkar's philosophy. The party considers only the liberal face of Ambedkar and it doesn't want to see the radical implications of Ambedkar's thought. It would like to consolidate its base by promising the most radical agenda in the context of a large number of Dalits leaning towards Dalit political parties centered around Ambedkar.

The action of Ambedkar embracing *Buddhism* is a complex act. This gives a chance for the Left-wingers to call him a conservative, since any identification with religion, in any form, is seen to be the opium of the masses by them. In a completely different move, the Hindu political parties may get theoretical advantage by Ambedkar's advocating of religion. They conveniently forget that he proposed Buddhism in place of Hinduism. In fact, this action can be used against the radical spirit of Ambedkar's philosophy by groups like the BJP, or Shivasena to portray Ambedkar as a *conservative* and appropriate his philosophy to their ends. They would also have the added advantage of keeping the Dalits away from other radical struggles.

Dalit masses projecting him as a demigod may involve many issues. The collective social and political aspirations of Dalits are culminated in associating with Ambedkar in a symbolic way. In the prevailing political atmosphere, Dalits are searching for their own identity and find that only the ideology of Ambedkar has the potential to liberate them.

However, the question of whether Ambedkar is a liberal, radical, or conservative thinker remains unsettled. One can see Ambedkar's association with the above streams of thinking, viz., liberal, radical and *conservative* through his writings. At same time he differentiates himself with these three dominant political traditions. Ambedkar may himself have struggled to find the new language to express the complexity of his thought. He was definitely cautious about his identification with the existing political language of his times. This often leads to a misunderstanding of his position. In contemporary times, once 'caste' got theoretically recognised and established as the Indian social reality, the established political and social theories got new meanings. Ambedkar as a thinker got prominence because of his scholarly conceptualisation of the institution of caste and its functioning in Indian society. He interpreted the Indian social world in order to change the lives of the Dalit masses who are the victims of *caste system*. The situation demands proper assessment of Ambedkar's *political philosophy* in relation to other prominent political streams of the time. Ambedkar is a real philosopher in the Marxian sense. For, he not only interpreted the world like a philosopher. He philosophised to change it.

In the post independent India, Dalit movement is one of the most influential and important social movements, which is fundamentally questioning the perceptions of ourselves and our paradigms of social reconstruction. Concerning *Dalit movement*, Ambedkar's philosophy is the source and inspiration. The debate and political activity of the movement is within the boundaries set by Ambedkar. He played an influential role on the movement both as an ideological thinker and as a political activist. He had a remarkable grasp of the dynamics of the Indian society. He should be considered as a crucial figure in the evolution of Indian political culture. Unfortunately, neither political nor intellectual community discovers in him a vision towards which India may move. There is a theoretical silence maintained by many about his views till recently. However, it is the *Dalit movement* with its powerful dissident voice against the upper caste hegemony that forces to revisit Ambedkar's views. Intense assertions of different communities, especially in post-Mandal era, have led to the study of Ambedkar's relevance in understanding caste as a central point in the projects of emancipation.

In contemporary times, *Dalit movement* emerged as a significant political struggle and provides a new vision to understand the Indian social reality. The term 'Dalit' refers to those who are economically and socially oppressed, or broken. It means the exploitation and oppression of masses economically, socially, culturally and politically in the name of *caste*. *Dalit movement* is an attempt to end Hindu traditional order and is made to bring into being a new world order. *Dalit movement* aims at annihilation of the *caste system*. The struggles aim at *self-respect* and *dignity* of the human being and social transformation. In other words, Dalit struggles are against the hegemony of upper castes for a casteless society. It is a movement that seeks to bring about a viable alternative.

Ambedkar's thought, as reflected in his writings and speeches has great importance in tracing the history and growth of social thought in India. It is necessary to understand the philosophy of Ambedkar which is the theoretical foundation for the Dalit movement. The core of political thinking of Ambedkar is contained in two of his statements— the rights are protected not by law but by social and moral conscience of society, and a democratic form of government presupposes a democratic form of society. He considers *democracy* essentially as a form of society of a more associated living and a social conscience is the only safeguard of all rights. The roots of *democracy* are to be searched in social relationships, in terms of associated life among the people who form a society. For him, social relationships are the key to *democracy*. Ambedkar is a *social democrat* in spirit and practice. His special contribution to political thought lies in his linking up *liberty*, *equality* and *fraternity* to the concept of social democracy, which in turn, he relates to democracy as a form of government. He further reminds the limitations of social democracy in everyday functioning. As he categorically stated while addressing the constituent assembly (November 25, 1949), "Political democracy can not last unless there lies at the base of it social democracy which means, a way of life which recognise *liberty*, *equality* and *fraternity* as the principles of life." In this sense he defined democracy as a form and method of government whereby revolutionary changes in the economic and social life of people are brought about without bloodshed.

In estimating Ambedkar's *political philosophy*, the study will consider the following questions: What is his conception of the human being and society? What are his conceptions of rights, freedom and justice that flow in both his thought and action? What are the cultural and historical roots of these conceptions in his thought? In what way does he connect democracy and social inequality? How does he resolve the question of individual and community? What kind of theory does he propose in bringing out the relationship between state and religion? How did he perceive the role of *Dalit movement* (Depressed class) in India's democratic future?

Ambedkar is influenced by all the major political traditions of his times. His political thought has emerged from the three grand traditions of political thought, i.e., liberal, conservative and radical. The unique feature about him is that he has transcended all these traditions. Though he was nurtured in the liberal tradition, he makes a difference from it. On many issues, he differs from liberal thinkers like Nehru. While embracing Buddhist religion, he seems to be conservative, but it is clearly evidenced that he is not conservative by his attack of *Gandhi* and the Hindu social order. At certain points, he seems to be radical (Marxist). But, throughout he maintains his differences with Marxist thought, particularly in understanding Indian society. However, the primary concern for Ambedkar is liberation of Dalits, the people of the lower strata of Indian society. He approached any political tradition from this point only. This has implications in providing the principles of reconstruction of Indian society. In other words, one feels that Ambedkar's political thought demands a whole new language and the existing political language fails short in assessing, or understanding his philosophy.

Dalit movements are rapidly spreading all over the country. We can see the politicisation of these people from *'untouchable'* to 'Dalit'. The study of Dalit movement has declared that Dalitisation of their society is an alternative to present social order. Challenges that face the movement in the present context are many. The *Dalit movement* has a long-standing problem of mobilisation and accommodation of the relatively less developed sub-castes within the category of Dalits. Another problem the Dalit movement has had to grapple with is the emergence of the Hindu right and the active support of some of the Dalit communities to it. Adding to this, the Dalits are further marginalised and opportunities are shrinking with the ongoing process of globalisation and privatisation of public sector. In this context, it is important to assess the usefulness of Ambedkar's philosophy for the future Dalit democratic movements.

Notes

1. Dasgupta, S.N., "Dogmas of Indian Philosophy", *Philosophical Essays*, New Delhi: Motilal Banarsidas, 1982, pp. 208-233.
2. Dayakrishna, "Three Myths about Indian Philosophy", *Indian Philosophy*: A Counter Perspective, New Delhi: Oxford University Press, 1991, pp. 3-15.
3. Bowes, Pratima. "What is Indian about Indian Philosophy?" S.S. Ramarao Pappu and R. Puligandla (Eds.), *Indian Philosophy: Past and Future*, New Delhi: Motilal Banarsidas, 1982, pp. 8-9.
4. Khilnani, Sunil. *Idea of India*., London: Penguin, 1999, p.154.
5. Rajaram Mohan Roy's Brahmasamaj (reformed Hinduism, and seeks reinterpretation of Upanishads), Dayanada Saraswati's 'going back to Vedas Gandhi's religion as a source for interconnectivity and for community life'.
6. Aurobindo's theory of evolution of spirit, Vivekananda-Hinduism not just as fulfillment of all other religions, but also as a fulfillment of all sciences'.
7. 'Fusion between modern and tradition', 'Meeting East and West', 'Truth is one, the wise call it by different names', 'Truth is God' (Gandhi), 'Integral Consciousness' (Aurobindo), 'Holistic approach' and 'Religious revolution' (J. Krishnamurti), 'Unity in diversity' (Radhakrishnan) 'Inner and outer' 'tolerance', 'scientific spirit' etc.-the language used by the contemporary modern philosophers.

2

Political Philosophy of Ambedkar

This chapter consists of three sections. The first section deals with an overview of political theory in the West with the specific purpose of providing a context to understand the *Political Philosophy of Ambedkar*. The second section exclusively focuses on the political philosophy of Ambedkar with specific emphasis on *democracy*, *caste* and *religion*. This study considers Ambedkar's enunciation of these concepts as radical because he is the first person to critically look at these institutions with an in-depth understanding of Western philosophical thinking. The third section tries to assess his contribution and relevance by various scholars and political parties. The assessment assumes critical importance in the context of intense debates over the meaning of Ambedkarite philosophy in the public realm.

Political Theory: An Overview

Let us have a brief look at major philosophical traditions of politics before we proceed into the *political philosophy* of Ambedkar. Political philosophers sought to explore social phenomena and political behaviour, (often in a historical context) as well as to clarify problematic concepts, evaluate existing institutions, and argue for social ideal. Political philosophy is about the critical reflection of politics and its practices. It is about the understanding of the governing principles of a society in a much more critical fashion. It tries to philosophise the values, principles, practices and institutions, which govern the society. Philosophers gave different interpretations about the meaning of public life and governing principles of good society. Socio-economic developments and the ensuing conflicts in society provide conditions for the emergence of new social and political theories. Political thought seems to spring from the political experience of both the thinker and his society. Political theory is enriched by the influence of both external and internal developments in society. Though rules and the institutions exist, human beings as conscious agents have the capacity to making choices either of conforming, or of changing them. Rules of politics are varied. We have to consider on what basis these rules are laid down. Political theory is nothing but the systematisation of moral and political judgments of our activities. Political activity is a managerial activity, which seeks to organise, or conciliate different interests, claims and demands of various wholes in a society by supervising its productive and distributive apparatus.

Classical political theory is a mixture of different kinds of inquiry, or speculation. One can distinguish three different impulses: philosophical, sociological and ideological. In case of classical thinkers like *Plato*, *Hobbes*, *Locke* and *Hegel*, their political speculation is philosophical. Each of these thinkers have tried to connect their conclusions about political organisation, or about the 'ends' of political life, with a wider philosophical system. They tried to derive political and social conclusions from more generalised beliefs about the nature of reality. In other words, political conclusions follow from, or are supported by more general, metaphysical principles. Traditional connection between philosophy and politics starts from the conception, that it is the task of philosophy to exhibit what is common between social and other 'spheres' of reality. Social thinking becomes ideological when it considers the moral argument about ends and ways of life and about the institutional conditions of good life. Ideological thinking tends to adopt global views of social structure and political action.

Morality of the society and the ways of functioning of institutions serve as source in deriving political theory. Political philosophy inquires into the ends of the State. What is morally necessary, or the morally justifiable ordering of political society? In this sense political philosophy has been considered as an extension of moral theory.

Political philosophy deals with the factual and descriptive accounts of political institutions and activities. It makes recommendations about the ideal ends that political activity should pursue and about the way political institutions should be designed in order to serve these ends, which may be called ideology. *Political philosophy* maintains analysis of substantive political discourses related to the factual statements of political science and the evaluative affirmation of ideology. The central concept of political science is that of State. Correlative with state is law. Positive law must have a state, or sovereign as its source and it is the first duty of a state to produce and maintain law. Satisfactory account of the nature of law must trace its complicated relations to morality, which serves both to supply law with content and to be a standard for criticism of it. The traditional natural theory is an attempt to expand this relationship.

Western social and political philosophers, since beginnings, in the writings of *Plato* and *Aristotle*, have been primarily concerned with a set of basic questions about the nature of authority and political obligation, the idea of liberty and its proper limitations, conceptions of the just and good society, and the best form of government. These problems naturally arise when the perceived interests of individuals, groups, or institutions came into conflict, particularly in the times of general social change and political instability when people became increasingly aware of new possibilities. Individuals, groups, or nations will demand more freedom, recognition of rights, greater justice in the distribution of goods, or a larger share in political decision-making. For the social contract theorists of the early modern period—*Hobbes*, *Locke*, *Rousseau* and others—the problem of political obligation was fundamental. They aimed to give a general account of why individuals are obliged to obey the laws of certain governments, at least under some conditions. The grounds of obligation is its *morality*, rationality, or common good? Freedom of an individual is a basic value and many thinkers tried to explain the restriction on *freedom*. Philosophers such as J.S. Mill have tried to give an account of what makes freedom valuable, and under what conditions. An adequate theory of this type can serve as the basis for rational and principled restraint when liberty conflicts with other basic values.

Justice is sometimes said to be the primary virtue of social institutions. It is one of the most significant respects in which legal and political arrangements, as well as economic systems and social hierarchies may be evaluated. Debate over the questions of distributive justice, especially, i.e., who is entitled to what share of benefits of social cooperation, and who must bear what burdens has always been in the forefront of Western political philosophy. Libertarians such as *Nozick* follow classical liberals (particularly Locke) in defending a right to private property based on conceptions of legitimate acquisition and voluntary transfer. The representative thinkers of egalitarians like *Rousseau*, *Rawls* and *Ronald Dworkin* emphasise the arbitrariness and deprivation, which appear to be a necessary part of such a system of 'natural liberty'. They argue for more equal distributions of wealth and opportunity through political means, based on conceptions of equal worth of human beings.[2]

Historically, Greek thought followed the Christian natural law. In the West, Christian natural law was undermined by the *individualism* of seventeenth century. This period was informed by the new vision of progress and freedom. Science had revolutionised people's life and thinking. Technological inventions brought in new wealth to society. Centralised and efficient nation states emerged in the world. Colonising efforts of Europeans were happening in large scale. Relationship between individual and god was replaced by the relationship between individual and individual as the foundation of social enquiry. This *individualism* became the basic characteristic of the subsequent liberal tradition. The idea of social initiative and social control surrendered to the idea of individual initiative and individual control. In simple terms, new material conditions gave birth to new social relationships and new philosophy was evolved to afford a rational justification for the new world which had come into being. This new philosophy became known as *liberalism*. *Liberalism* acquired different flavours in different national cultures. Several Non-Western countries from 1950s onwards, have their own versions of mixed *liberalism*, not only borrowed from the West but also blended with their own cultural practices. Later theories of politics tried to articulate from the point of community, or individual in relation to community.

The individualist position is 'radical', because of the implicit commitment to subject *all* beliefs and institutions *to review, according none a privileged status of critical immunity*. The *communitarian* position is '*conservative*' in the sense that it accepts the validity of central categories of moral self-description that are entrenched within the practices and institutions of society.

Diverse set of philosophical traditions has justified the liberal conception of man and society. *Individualism* as a basic theoretical position starts at least as far back as *Hobbes*. Although his conclusions are scarcely being called liberal, his postulates are highly individualistic. He discarded the traditional *concepts of society*, *justice*, and *natural law*. He deduced the political rights and obligations from the interests and will of dissociated individuals. *Individualism* of another sort emphasising the equal moral worth of every human being was clearly fundamental in puritan political thinking. This individualism in a different way was developed by John Locke.[3] In *Locke's* theoretical scheme individual is somewhat placed as a moral being rather than a crude individual. All these theories are related to the struggles for a more liberal state.

The doctrines of utilitarian theories in eighteenth and nineteenth century were the restatements of individualist principles that were already worked out in seventeenth century. *Bentham's utilitarian* theory built on Hobbes. The Benthamite assumption that man in his political relations was and should be treated as a calculator of his own interests and that this exhausted his nature as political man, has been perceived as a perversion of the fundamental liberal insight of an earlier tradition. *J.S. Mill* also attacked the *Bentham's utilitarianism* from this vantage ground.[4] The liberal individualism of *Bentham* identified itself with narrowly selfish and narrowly rational *teleology*. There was an attempt to expose the weakness of liberal individualism. It is true that one would not expect fundamental political principles of seventeenth century to be entirely sufficient for a changed and more complex twentieth century world. Still one could build upon the earlier principles if they corresponded to the needs, aspirations and capacities of modern man. However, this is considered as a serious problem with the liberal theory of earlier version. This theory fails to recognise the sense of moral worth of the individual and the necessity to combine it with a sense of moral value of community. In some measure this has been presented in Puritan and Lockean theory. *Locke* refused to reduce all social relations to market relations and all morality to market morality. He would not entirely let go of the traditional natural law. There are several attempts to consider the desirable values of individualism and by discarding its excesses. *J.S. Mill* and *T.H. Green's* idealism are examples in this direction.

The difficulties in liberal theory lies in its basic foundations of seventeenth century individualism and its quality of possessiveness. The possessive quality lies in the conception of the individual as essentially the proprietor of his own person, or capacities owing nothing to society. The individual was seen neither as a moral whole, nor as a part of a larger social whole, but as a proprietor of himself. The basic assumption of possessive individualism that man is free and human by virtue of his sole proprietorship of his own person, and that human society is essentially a series of market relations, was deeply embedded in seventeenth century foundations. This theory may correspond with the market society of seventeenth century. In this relation of ownership, the actual freedom and actual prospect of realising their full potentialities lead backwards to recognising the nature of the individual. The individual, it was thought, is free in as much as he is proprietor of his person and capacities. The human essence is freedom from dependence on the wills of others, and freedom is the function of possession. Society becomes the web of free equal individuals related to each other as proprietors of their own capacities. Society consists of relations of exchange between proprietors. Political society becomes a calculated device for the protection of this property and for the maintenance of an orderly relation of exchange. We could not say that seventeenth century concepts of freedom, rights, obligation and *justice* are all entirely derived from the concept of possession. But it can be shown that they were powerfully shaped by it.

The inconsistency lies inherently in the market society itself. Market society automatically brings the class differentiations. The propertied class would like to hold power over the subordinate classes. Men no longer saw themselves fundamentally equal in an inevitable subjection to the determination of market. Alternatives emerged for the market system. Articulation of proletarian politics gave a serious blow to the liberal politics. There are altogether different assumptions about man and society. The community has replaced individual. Marxist theory aims at the radical change in society and its human relations. Human society has seen from the perspective of the class, considers human being as primarily a producer. His relations are determined by his involvement in social production. Other than the Marxist notion there is a conservative political theory which likes to see society from the point of view of community. *Conservatism* has reverence for tradition, religion and age old custom. *Edmund Burke* is the one of the examples for conservative tradition. Burke more than any thinker of eighteenth century approached the political tradition with a sense of religious reverence.

Rousseau's nostalgia for city state and *Burke* reverence for the national tradition can be considered in the phases of development of a new cult of society which was replacing the old cult of individual. The conservative view of politics is known as politics of tradition. The state in particular and society in general must operate with respect to traditions and customs. The rights of the groups are acknowledged in that particular society. Conservative perspective works within the limits of the given order accepting forms of political action within the structural framework of existing institutions.

Conservative theory of politics is known as politics of imperfection. It finds limitations with human beings and believes that human beings will be unable to create a social order through their own spontaneous efforts. People are inherently greedy and selfish. To restrain them there is a need for a state. The power is state. State plays a central role in conservative thought. It is the backbone of social order and authority, the guarantor of social hierarchy. As per the conservative views, the inherent imperfections of human nature make a strong state necessary. It is needed to control the anti-social impulses of the individual. State has been seen as a crucial institution necessary to prevent society from dissolving into disorder and chaos. The conservative thinkers consider the forms of inequality and privilege as ineradicable and necessary elements of society. 'Inequality of function, role and power is as necessary to the social order as a whole as to the family'. According to conservative thought without hierarchical structure no society can survive. As per the traditional conservative perspective, social order is not and can never be achieved spontaneously by the free play of individual activities as claimed by liberals and anarchists. *Social order* has to be maintained through the strong leadership of those who hold positions of political responsibility. It does not mean that state is the only agency which maintains social order. Conservatives stress the importance of tradition, custom and of network of longstanding groups and associations, all prerequisites of social order.

In the late1970s, political scientist *Fred R. Dallmayr* reiterated the statement of *Peter Laslett*, "the great tradition of theoretical literature stretching from *Hobbes* to Bosanquet had been broken and that for the moment, anyway, political philosophy is dead".[5] This is not exactly true. But it shows there is no break in development of political philosophy and existing theories got some setbacks. Of course, there are struggles of 70s, students, revolt and Vietnam debacle changed the purpose and meaning of public life. Political thought shares the affliction of philosophy. True philosophy makes us to learn again to see the world. It seeks to render political life intelligible, political theory has to remain attentive to the concrete sufferings and predicaments of people and cannot pretend prematurely to knowledge, or understanding. The crisis in political philosophy may be understood with the changed socio-economic developments and the unrelatedness of intellectual to the politics. In twentieth century, Western political philosophy is marked with its defence of liberal democracy and legacy of civil rights against totalitarian, or repressive forces. The economic practices and scientific rationality of West got different meaning in the developing nations. In recent times, the culmination of Western science and economics leading towards dominance over other parts of the world invite competition and confrontation at global level. This situation has compelled the West to rethink and reformulate its central premises of its philosophy, and its conception of 'reason'. And at the same time, there is a need to critically understand what constitutes 'subjectivity' and its cognitive activity. This dilemma seems to be aptly captured by *Fred Dallmayr*, "In the domain of political thought, the contemporary dilemma can be phrased broadly in terms of the relationship between 'contract' and 'community'. Society is of collectives and generates political community.[6] Far from involving only the aspect of inter-subjective, or inter-individual contracts, a revision, or modification of *individualism* in the light of communal bonds necessitates a general reconsideration of man's relation to the world and nature-a reconsideration that inevitably conjures up the peril of objectivism and naturalism. Contemporary political theory appears precariously lodged at the cross roads of liberal individualism and post-individualist communalism.[7]

Christian Bay elaborates this in his article 'From Contract to Community', he links up the major predicaments of post-industrial society with the basic assumptions and preferences of 'individualistic contract liberalism' as inaugurated by *Hobbes* and *Locke* and it manifested in different forms. He notes that liberals have 'persistently tended to cut the citizen off from the person', putting on their pedestal 'a cripple of a man' without a 'moral, or political nature' and without 'moorings in any real community'.[8]

Political Philosophy of Ambedkar

Ambedkar's philosophy is primarily *ethical and religious*. He thoroughly explored the Indian traditions and its philosophical systems in a unique way. He developed political concepts like *democracy*, *justice*, state and rights from his understanding of Indian society and the functioning of its institutions on the moral grounds. He is very critical of the institution of *caste*, which influences all the spheres of individual's life and the Indian society as a whole. He further discusses how individual is related to society and how individual's freedom is limited by other social forces. He is critical of authoritarian Hindu social order and argued in favour of democratic society. He probed into the moral and social foundations of India and gave new meaning to the lives of disadvantaged people. His was a rationale approach. Reason plays a role in his writings and speeches. The methodology he used is very scientific rather speculative. He was influenced by the assumptions of *modernity*. He is well informed in many areas of Indian history, polity, culture, anthropology and philosophy. He quotes many thinkers in his writings those who have influenced him.

He was influenced by the ideas of *John Dewey*, the pragmatic American and the teacher of him. The *Fabian Edwin R.A. Seligman* had considerable impact on his thought. He often quoted Edmund *Burke*, the British, *conservative* thinker though we can't brand

Ambedkar as *conservative*. Ambedkar's notion of liberty comes close to *T.H. Green*.

It is very difficult to fit him into dominant political traditions like *liberalism*, *Marxism* and *conservatism*. He himself finds difficulty in explaining his political position. It doesn't mean that there is no consistency in his political thinking. The problem lies only in explaining his thought in existing political vocabulary. He critically engaged with *liberalism*, *Marxism* and *Gandhism*. He describes himself as a *progressive radical* and occasionally as a *'progressive conservative'*. One thing is clear that he would like to be a progressive, and distinguish himself from liberals and *communists* depending on the case.

The notion of community is central to his thinking.

To say that individuals make up society is trivial; society is always composed of classes. It may be exaggeration to assert the theory of class conflict, but the existence of definite classes in society is a fact... an individual in a society is always a member of a class. A *caste* is an enclosed class. Brahmins created caste and it is extended to other servile classes. *Caste* is *endogamous* unit and also a communal unit. His political theory was premised on moral community. It was as an ideal to be realised. Hinduism is not qualified to be a community. He was very much critical about the Hindu social order. *Buddhism* was projected as the ideal having the value of community grounding on morality. He argues that *Buddhism* attempted to found society on the basis of 'reason' and 'morality'.

On Democracy

Ambedkar had a lengthy discussion on democratic form of government in his writings. His conception of democracy is different from the parliamentary democracy of Western Europe. *Democracy* came with the principles of liberalism. His conception of democracy makes difference with parliamentary forms in a significant way.

The Government of human society has undergone some very significant changes. To change from autocracy to parliamentary democracy, bloody struggles were fought in the world. It is believed that every human being will have the right to liberty, property and pursuit of happiness. Parliamentary democracy has all the marks of a popular government, a government of people, by the people and for the people. Ambedkar considered the problems and expressed discontent against the parliamentary democracy in the nations like Italy, Germany, Russia, Spain and some other European nations in proposing the parliamentary democracy in India. Ambedkar finds reasons for the failure of parliamentary democracy that 'parliamentary democracy gives no free hand to dictatorship and that is why it became a discredited institution in the countries like Italy, Spain and Germany which readily welcomed dictatorships'.[9] The nations that are opposing dictatorship and pledged to democracy, too, find their discontent with democracy. First, the parliamentary democracy began with equality of political rights in the form of equal suffrage. There are very few countries having parliamentary democracy that have not adopted adult suffrage. It has progressed by expanding the notion of equality of political rights to equality of social and economic opportunity. It has recognised that corporations, which are anti-social in purpose, cannot hold state at bay. With all this, 'the reason for discontent is due to the realisation that it has failed to assure to the masses the right to liberty, property, or the pursuit of happiness. The causes for this failure may be found either in wrong ideology, or wrong organisation, or in both.'[10]

He elaborated this point by pointing out the fault with both wrong ideologies and the bad organisation in carrying the ideals of democracy. The idea of freedom of contract is one of the responsible factors for parliamentary democracy in terms of ideology. Parliamentary democracy took no notice of economic inequalities and didn't care to examine the result of freedom of contract on the parties to the contract, in spite of the fact that they were unequal in bargaining power. It didn't mind if the freedom of contract gave the strong opportunity to defraud the weak. The result is that parliamentary democracy in standing out as a protagonist of liberty has continuously added to economic wrongs of the poor, downtrodden and disinherited class.'[11]

The second wrong ideology which has vitiated parliamentary democracy is the failure to realise that political democracy can not succeed where there is no social and economic democracy.[12] He illustrated this point by comparing the collapse of parliamentary democracy in the countries of Italy, Germany and Russia with England and USA. He felt that there was a greater degree of economic and social democracy in the latter countries than existed in the former. 'Social and economic democracy are the tissues and fiber of a political democracy. The tougher the tissue and the fiber, the greater the strength of the body.[13]

Democracy is another name for *equality*. Parliamentary democracy developed a passion for liberty. It never made even nodding acquaintance with equality. It failed to realise the significance of equality and didn't even strike a balance between *liberty* and *equality*, with the result the liberty swallowed equality and has made democracy a name and farce.

More than the bad ideology, bad organisation is responsible for failure of democracy. All political societies get divided into two classes—the rulers and the ruled. This is almost stratified that rulers are always drawn from ruling class and the class that is ruled never become the ruling class. This happens because generally people do not see that they govern themselves. They are content to establish a government and leave it to govern them. This explains why parliamentary democracy has never been a government of the people, or by the people and why it has been in reality a government of hereditary subject class by a hereditary ruling class. It is this vicious organisation of political life which had made parliamentary democracy such a dismal failure.[14]

Ambedkar is not a blind supporter of parliamentary *democracy* as a governing system. First of all, he critically evaluates the functioning of parliamentary *democracy* in European nations. In adopting this model in nations like India, he reminds the problems involved for the real functioning of parliamentary *democracy*. Historically, it is a fact that in every country there exists governing classes and servile classes and there is a continuous struggle for power in between these classes. The governing class finds it easy to maintain its supremacy over its servile class through its power and prestige. Adult suffrage and the frequent elections is not a hurdle for the governing class to attain power and authority. On the other hand the servile classes regards them members of governing class as their natural leaders and volunteer to elect them as their rulers by considering themselves as inferior. It is wrong to believe that democracy and self-government is automatically became realities of life. In fact, the existing governing class is inconsistent with democracy and self-government and made all its efforts to retain its power to govern. Ambedkar felt that self-government and *democracy* become real not when the constitution based on adult suffrage comes into existence but when the governing class loses its power to capture the power to govern. In some of the countries the servile classes may succeed in ousting the governing class from the seat of authority just by adult suffrage. In some other countries the governing class may be so deeply entrenched that the servile classes will need other safeguards besides adult suffrage to achieve the same end.[15]

Ambedkar accused the Western writers that they are superficial and have not provided the realistic view of democracy. They superficially touched the constitutional morality, adult suffrage and frequent elections as the be-all and end-all of *democracy*. Ambedkar proposed a written constitution for the effective democracy. The habits of constitutional morality may be essential for the maintenance of a constitutional form of government. He puts more emphasis on moral society and its custom than the written legal law in governing its people. He heavily invested on social morality for effective functioning of the democratic form of government. He reminds us very often, in devising the *constitution* one has to keep in mind that the principle aim of *constitution* must be to dislodge the governing class from its position and to prevent it from remaining as a governing class forever.[16]

Evolution of Indian Democracy and Untouchables as a Political Subject

The Constitution of India is evolved from the time of *colonial* rule. It has undergone various changes with the demands of various groups of Indian society. In the colonial time after the Government of India Act of 1919, British government appointed a royal commission in 1927 to look into the working of Indian Constitution under the chairmanship of Sir John Simon. This is popularly known as Simon Commission. The Commission invited the representative Indians to the Round Table Conference at London, to settle the new Constitution to India. The Congress party boycotted the Simon Commission in its first power to capture the power to govern. In some of the countries the servile classes may succeed in ousting the governing class from the seat of authority just by adult suffrage. In some other countries the governing class may be so deeply entrenched that the servile classes will need other safeguards besides adult suffrage to achieve the same end.

The *Depressed Classes* Association of India gave evidence before Simon Commission and most of them pleaded for separate electorates for the depressed classes. On behalf of the Bhahishkrit Hitakarini Sabha, Dr. Ambedkar submitted a memorandum to demand for joint electorate with reservation of seats for the *depressed classes.*[17]

Ambedkar argued for joint electorates for *depressed classes* but at the same time he opposed territorial electorates and separate electorates. "Territorial electorate and separate electorates are the two extremes which must be avoided in any scheme of representation that may be devised for the introduction of a democratic form of government in this undemocratic country. The golden mean is the system of joint electorates with reserved seats. Less than that would be insufficient, more than that would defeat the ends of good government."[18]

The Round Table Conference at London invited leaders of Hindu liberals, Muslim representatives, representatives of Sikhs, the *Hindu Maha Sabha*, rulers of various Indian states and Ambedkar and Rao Bahadur Srinivasan from depressed classes were also invited. Ambedkar effectively negotiated with British government the demand of *depressed classes* for consideration in making the future constitution of India. This was the first occasion that *depressed classes* were identified as a special political category in governing the future government. On the other hand, Congress abused those leaders who are cooperated with British government and showed its anger against leaders of *depressed classes* as the agents of British. In fact, the Congress and its leadership from the beginning didn't want to consider depressed classes as a separate category and negated their claims.

However, Congress never took the issue of *depressed classes* seriously. It was afraid that it would lose the political consolidation of the nation, if it presses on the issue of caste. This can be seen from its programmes. In the initial stage, the liberal social elite of Congress felt for the social reform programmes and later the agitation of Congress against the British taking up in its peak stage, they gave up the social reform issue in their advancement of political struggles. If one touched the issues of *caste* it may have bad implication on Congress, they therefore either deliberately ignored, or argued for the issue to be deferred to a future date. One may also find this attitude with the communist movement of India of early stage. Communists are claimed for the working class and mostly its leaders are liberal upper caste people. They considered that to talk about caste was anti-modern.

In the Round Table Conference, Ambedkar had not only proved himself as strong nationalist and revolutionary of India, he had effectively represented one fifth population of India, the poorest of the poor who were half-fed and half-nude. He questioned the *British rule* in the round table conference in relation to the *depressed classes*. In his own words, "Before British, we were in the loathsome condition due to our *untouchability*. Has the British government done anything to remove it? Before the British, we could not draw water from the village well. Has the British government secured us the right to draw water from the well? Before the British, we could not enter temple. Can we enter now? Before the British, we were denied entry into the police force. Does the British government admit us into the force? Before the British, we were not allowed to serve in military. Is that career now open to us? To none of these questions can we give an affirmative answer. Our wrongs have remained as open sores and they have not been righted, although 150 years of *British rule* have rolled away."[19]

Ambedkar further pointed out, the *British rule* in India supported the capitalists who were denying the workers a living wage and decent conditions of work and which did realise that the landlords were squeezing the masses dry. Also, he realised that *British rule* did not remove social evils that blighted the lives of the down trodden classes for several decades. The legal powers were not invoked to remove these evils, it did not amend the existing code of social and economic life, because it was afraid that its intervention would rise to resistance.

Therefore, we must have governments in which the men in power will give their undivided allegiance to the best interests of the country. We must have a government in which men in power, knowing where obedience will end and resistance will begin, will not be afraid to amend the social and economic code of life which the dictates of justice and expediency so urgently called for.[20]

Ambedkar upheld the demand for Dominion status, but expressed doubts as to whether the depressed classes would be heir to it unless the political machinery for the new constitution was of a special make. He felt that no constitution is workable which is not acceptable to majority of the people. He opined, "Let the consent of people and not the accident of logic be touchstone of your new Constitution, if you desire that it should be worked."

The Social Precedes the Political

In most of the speeches and writings of Ambedkar, the central theme is social reformism. He often debated and confronted on the issue of precedence of social over political issues. Politics have to be necessarily connected to the social issues. The very foundations of democracy lie in associated living in society. On the issue of giving primacy to social over political, he differs with Congress and socialists. This is well reflected in all his writings in general and his writings '*Annihilation of caste*' and '*What Congress and Gandhi have done to untouchables*' in particular.

Ambedkar pointed out that initially *Congress* party mentioned in its agenda, the social reform along with political reform. The leaders of Indian National Congress felt that national movement should not be exclusively political but that side by side with the consideration of political questions, questions affecting Indian social economy should also be discussed. They felt the need to revitalise Hindu society by removing all social evils and social wrongs. To discuss the social issues Congress resolved to form Indian national social conference (1886). Later social reform party had formed a separate organisation of its own to discuss the many social evils, which festered Hindu society. They were not satisfied with the *Congress* attitude of completely dissociating itself from the questions of social reform.[21] Before 1895, there are two schools among congressmen on the issue of social reform versus political reform. The former did recognise the need of social reform but thought that the Congress session was not proper platform to it. The later denied that there was need for social reform and challenged the view that there cannot be political reform without social reform.[22] In 1895, in the Congress meeting at Pune, the anti-social reform group of Congress under the leadership of Tilak threatened to burn the Congress pandal if the Congress allowed it to be used by the social conference. The Pro-Social reforms of *Congress* were not prepared to fight its opponents. The untouchables organised a demonstration against the Congress and burned its effigy.[23] After 1895, Congress kept away from the agenda of social reform. This coincided with the new phase of active consolidation of Congress through mass mobilisation while the earlier Congress was limited to intellectual activity.

With the entry of *Gandhi* into Indian politics in 1919, the Congress became totally different from the early times and it became a mass organisation. By 1922 Congress was totally transformed by *Gandhi*. The controversy over the issues of social vs. political, the *political reform* faction supported the National Congress and social reform faction supported the social conference. In course of time social reform faction lost its battle. Ambedkar tried to find out the reasons for it. The social reform could be understood in two senses, in one sense it is the 'reform of Hindu family' and in the other sense it is the 'reorganisation and reconstruction of the Hindu society'. The social reform in Hindu family concerned the issues like widow remarriage, child marriage etc., whereas the reconstruction of Hindu society relates to the issues like abolition of the caste system. The social conference consisted of mostly enlightened high caste Hindus that they were concerned mainly with reform of high caste Hindu family and they did not feel the necessity for agitating for the abolition of caste, or had not the courage to agitate for it.[24] He comes to a conclusion that this may be the reason for the loss of reform faction.

Further, Ambedkar continued that political constitution must take note of social organisation and the social forces. The political reformers entrusted with the making of the *Constitution*, found it impossible to ignore the problem arising out of the prevailing social order. The religious and social problems definitely had a bearing on political constitutions. It can be seen in history that political revolutions have always been preceded by social and religious revolutions.[25]

Apart from *Congress*, Ambedkar is also critical about the socialists of India. They apply economic interpretation of history. Everything is reduced to economy. According to *Marxism* property is the only source of power. Economic reform by equalisation of property must have precedence over every other kind of reform, either social, or political. Ambedkar contested the socialist position that economic power is the only power. He identifies there are other sources of power, social status and religion. Religion, social status and property are all sources of power and authority, which one man has, to control the liberty of another.[26] He further considers that if the source of power and domination, at any given society, is in social and religious life then social reform and religious reform must be accepted as the necessary sort of reform.

Ambedkar posed a question to Indian socialists, "can you have economic reform without first bringing about a reform of the social order? Can it be said that proletariat of India recognise no distinctions except that of rich and poor? Can it be said that the poor in India recognise no such distinctions of *caste* or creed, high or low? How can there be a revolution if the proletariat cannot present a united front?"[27] The socialists had no option to make socialism a definite reality; they must recognise the problem of social reform as fundamental. "He will be compelled to take account of *caste* after revolution if he doesn't take account of it before revolution...turn in any direction you like, caste is the monster that crosses your path. You cannot have political reform; you cannot have economic reform, unless you kill this monster."[28]

Ambedkar argues that Hindu society doesn't have the qualification to be called as a 'society'. Men do not become a society by living in physical proximity any more. Similarity in habits and customs, beliefs and thoughts is not enough to constitute men into society. Men constitute a society because they have things, which they possess in common. To have similar thing is totally different from possessing things in common.

Men possess things in common with one another is by being in communication with one another. Society continues to exist by communication, indeed in communication. To make it concrete, it is not enough if men act in a way, which agrees with acts of others. Men should participate, or share in common activity to have any social activity. The *caste system* prevents common activity and by preventing common activity it has prevented the Hindus from becoming a society with a unified life and a consciousness of its own being.[29]

Hindu society lives in isolation and exclusiveness. As the Hindu society characterised by its caste system, it prevents any solidarity. It has anti-social spirit. Caste kills the public spirit. Caste has destroyed the sense of public charity. Caste has made public opinion impossible. A Hindu's public is his caste. Virtue has become caste-ridden and morality has become caste-bound.

Ambedkar has a vision of ideal society that reflected in most of his writings. An ideal society should be mobile and it should be full of channels for conveying a change—taking place in one part to other parts. In an ideal society there should be many interests consciously communicated and shared. There should be varied and free points of contact with other modes of association. In simple terms, Ambedkar viewed that an ideal society would be based on *liberty*, *equality* and *fraternity*.[30]

Ambedkar favours religion that stands for reason. He felt Hindu religion need to undergo a reform. *Caste* is a natural outcome of certain religious beliefs, which have the sanction of *shastras*. To abolish the sanctity and sacredness of caste, one has to destroy the authority of the *shastras* and *Vedas*. One has to destroy the religion of *sruti* and smriti. Ambedkar not only proposed that religion stands, for reason, but also tried to link up religion with the governing principle of politics. He convinced the necessity of religion. He outlined the religion with a rule of reform. One interesting suggestion he made, in case priesthood among Hindus was not abolished, at least make the priest a subject of state. A priest should be the servant of the state and should be subject to the disciplinary action by state in the matter of his morals, beliefs and worship, in addition to his being subject along with other citizens to the ordinary law of the land.[31]

Ambedkar justifies his argument in favour of religion by borrowing ideas from *Burke* and *John Dewey. Edmund Burke* had opposed the principle of change embodied in the *French revolution*. He considered the *French revolution* to be against the will of the god. Ambedkar was influenced by Burke's writings. At the same time, Ambedkar knows the limitation of the arguments of Burke. While Ambedkar condemned religion of rules, he understood the necessity of religion. He agrees with Burke that, 'true religion is the foundation of society, the basis on which all true civil government rests, and both their sanction.[32] Following the line of Burke, Ambedkar found true religion to be the basis of society and religion should be in consonance with *liberty*, *equality,* and *fraternity*. In short, the true religion must be democratic in all its acts and forms. These very ideals may derive from the indigenous traditions. This may provide complete change in the fundamental notions of life and its values. It brings the change in outlook and in attitude towards men and things.

John Dewey is the well known thinker of pragmatism, happened to be the teacher of Ambedkar and had a great influence on him. Keeping himself in tune with his teacher, Ambedkar pointed out that Hindus felt that there is no point in conserving the whole social heritage. What is useful and helpful in any tradition, or past may be preserved for the future society. What is required for the democratic and enlightened society may converse and transmit for future generation. We should be selective in inventing our traditions. He quotes Dewey, 'the study of past products will not help us to understand the present. Knowledge of the past and its heritage is of great significance when it enters into the present, but not otherwise'.

Further he suggests to Hindus that there is nothing fixed, eternal, *sanatan*. Everything is changing, that change is the law of life for individuals as well as for society. In a changing society, there must be a constant revolution of old values and the Hindus must realise that if there are standards to measure the acts of men there must also be readiness to revise those standards.

Theorising Caste in India

Caste has been for a many centuries a real and active part of Indian life. *Caste* has been a dynamic force in Indian life and thought and is a multidimensional reality. In the ancient times, reverence for certain generalised caste ideals is extolled in important scriptural writing. It does not mean that single static system of caste has dominated since ancient times. The institutions and beliefs which are now often described as the elements of traditional caste were taken shape in the early eighteenth century in the Hindu heartland of Gangetic Upper India. This is the period of rapid regional state building, which accompanied the collapse of Mughal rule and the expansion of Western power in the subcontinent. From the early nineteenth century onwards, *British rule* significantly expanded and sharpened these norms and conventions, building many manifestations of caste language and ideology into its structure of authoritative government. One can see the importance of caste affinities in the political arena from the time of colonialism. With the practices of representative government, from the early election to the elections of independent India caste has been an effective tool and resource for the creation of common interests across the boundaries of region, language, faith and economic status. It is true that the assertion of caste has made possible to build broad allegiances cutting across the boundaries of region, faith, language and economic status of India. And at the same time caste principles have often provided the means of exclusion, disempowering, or subjugating others.

There are many theories and debates about the caste system. The people of lower caste origin are often significantly poorer, less well educated, more inclined towards unprestigious forms of folk religion, and even physically dark-skinned than those claiming superior caste ranks. By this one cannot come to conclusions about the features of the caste. It needs elaborate study to understand the origin and functioning of the caste. For anthropologists like *F.G. Bailey* (1957), caste was not a unique moral, or religious system. It was merely a more elaborate form of social stratification to be found in many other societies: the true basis of the distinction between those of low and high caste was differential access to political and economic resources.[33]

The question of caste whether it is virtuous, or destructive element in Indian life is very much debated in late nineteenth and early twentieth century. In the early nineteenth century, this is debated in the Sanskrit and vernacular languages. *Christian missionaries* and Western Orientalists had claims of superiority of their faith and social values over the caste Hindu India. They posed that value system they represented got rooted in traditions of casteless universalism. There are many conceptions about the origin and functions of caste in India. One of the prominent views is of anthropologist *Dumont* as it explained the ethnographic view of *caste system* in *Homo hierarchicus* (1970). It basically explains the Brahman and Kshatriya relationship within the *varna* hierarchy—that *Dumont* derives from early Hindu texts. The structure of Indian society, as concretely manifested in its contemporary villages, is thus revealed as fundamentally unchanged since ancient times. *Dumont* holds that the political and economic domains of social life in India are encompassed by the 'religious' life. The religious principle becomes articulated in terms of the opposition of purity and impurity. For *Dumont*, the Brahmin represents the religious principle, in as much as the Brahman represents the highest form of purity attainable by Hindus. The king, while important and powerful, represents the political domain, and is accordingly inferior to, and encompassed by, the Brahman. *Dumont* has suggested that caste is fundamentally religious, and that religious principles actualise themselves in the domain of purity and pollution. Dumont's position in many ways caricatures the *Orientalist* assumption that India is the spiritual East, devoid of history, untouched by the politics of oriental despotism. Critics of *Dumont* have often accepted his basic epistemological premises, but then reversed them. They take materialist perspective and view social relations in India in terms of power, pure and simple. Some of the thinkers who are influenced by ethno-sociological approach to study India, has suggested that this separation of religion from politics, like many other dichotomies in Western social sciences, is inappropriate at the level of ideological (or cultural) analysis in Indian social thought (Appadurai 1981, Dirks 1982).

Not only is there no fundamental ontological separation of a 'religious' from 'political' domain, but religious institutions and activities are fundamental features of what we describe here as the political systems. Kings derive much of their power from worship; temples are institutions in the formation of social communities. There are not two distinct forms of power, *secular* power had by kings and sacred power had by Brahmans. Kings and Brahmans are both privileged but by different forms of divinity in a world in which all beings were, however distantly, generated from the same ontological source. Dirks argued that colonial sociology represented the 18th century as decadent, and all legitimate Indian politics as past. Under *colonialism*, caste was appropriated, and in many respects reinvented, by British (1989). However, the British were able to change caste because *caste* continued to be permeable to political influence.

Bayly argues that both the old idea of timeless India and the newer revisionism which almost claims that *colonialism* alone made India into a caste society are erroneous. In fact, both in precept and practice, caste as a rigid and hierarchical system had long been established at major, Brahman-dominated centers of Hindu scholarship. 'Traditional' Indian society was not created out of nothing by *British rule*, but it was 'consolidated' by it. And as it was through the combined effect of colonial institutions and discourse, as *Dirks* argues, that caste was made into peculiarly rigid social phenomenon detached from political processes, and 'a specifically Indian form of civil society'.

M.N. Srinivas (1957) argued that caste had been strengthened in the context of modern politics: 'the power and activity of caste has increased in proportion as political power passed increasingly to the people from rulers. Although this strengthening had started in the colonial period, it greatly accelerated after independence in 1947. It is a 'transition from structure to substance'.

Ambedkar's Conception of Caste

Ambedkar identified *caste* as an important institution, in understanding the Indian society. In evolving his political theory, one could not ignore the role of caste system in India. No political theory is possible without understanding the caste system. Ambedkar is the first thinker who systematised the conception of *caste* in an analytical way. Earlier discussions on caste are ethnographic and descriptive in nature. His approach is more political rather than ethnographical. He made an attempt to understand the origin and functioning of caste in order to understand the lives of the victims of the caste system. He understood that whole Indian social system has caste as its foundation. The beliefs, customs, knowledge are centered on caste system. All the human activities are determined by the *caste*. *Caste* has social, political and economical implications. Misusing the caste system, the so-called majoritarian religion Hinduism could not withstand on its own. In simple terms, caste is the primary institution of Indian society and other institutions like family, state, nation, and school are directly or indirectly related, or influenced by it.

Most of his writing occupied the discussions on *caste*. Some of the important works of Ambedkar in this regard are-*Castes in India-their origin, genesis and mechanism, Annihilation of caste, Who were the Shudras and how they came to be the fourth Varna in Indo-Aryan society? The untouchables: Who were they and how they became untouchables?* He discussed the origin and functioning of caste in an elaborate way. There is a significant change in understanding caste over the period of his writings. The improvement on the conception of caste can be seen as his journey from anthropologist to political scientist. Initially, he argued that the characteristic of caste was endogamy superimposed on exogamy in a shared cultural ambience. He suggested that such evils as sati, child marriage and prohibition of widow marriage were the outcome of the institution of caste. First of all, the Brahmins as endogamous community gave rise to the system of caste. Ambedkar continued to emphasise the endogamous characteristic of *caste* but roped in other features such as the division of labour, absence of inter-dining and principle of birth which he had earlier largely absorbed within endogamy. He also found that caste name is an important feature which keeps the solidarity of caste intact. He increasingly argued that graded inequality is the normative anchor of the *caste system*. Graded inequality restricts the reach of equality to members of the caste, at the most. Ambedkar thought *caste* as an essential feature of Hindu religion.

It is generally understood that Indo-Aryan society of ancient India was based upon *Varna* system. The society is divided into *Brahmins*,

Kshtriyas, Vaishyas and *Sudras* based on the principle of labour and heredity. Some of the scholars would like to argue as *chaturvarna* system based on economic theory of division of labour and also the *varna* system is scientific. In later days, when the people affected by the *varna* hierarchy contested it, individuals were defined by their acquired qualities (*guna*) but not by birth. However, Ambedkar refutes the *chaturvarna* system and argued that it as not only divided the society but also divided the labourers. Further, this *chaturvarna* is opposed to natural law and spirit of human development.

Ambedkar argued that initially there were only three *varnas* in Indo-Aryan society. The *shudras* were not a separate *varna* but were part of *Kshtriya varna*. There was a constant feud between *sudra* kings and Brahmins. Brahmins were insulted and tortured by these *Kshtriya* kings. Ambedkar believed that Brahmins began to take revenge upon *Kshtriyas* through 'divinity' and 'infinity' ideas, which later on came to be attached to religious laws continued in course of time as sacred laws. Brahmins hatred towards sudras culminated in their refusal to invest the sudras with sacred thread. The sacred thread in ancient India presupposed a higher social and economic status. Owing to the loss of sacred thread, the sudras were socially degraded and demoted to the rank of the fourth *varna*. Ambedkar illustrates this point through the examples from Hindu mythology.

Ambedkar further probed into how the practice of untouchability came into existence. In other words how the *panchama varna,* or *avarnas* came into existence. He gave a detailed historical account of origin of *untouchability*. He explains first those untouchables are not of a different race. There is no racial difference between Hindus and the *untouchables*. Just as untouchability has no racial basis, so also has it no occupational basis. The distinction between the Hindus and *untouchables* in its original form, before the advent of untouchablity was the distinction between 'tribesmen' and 'broken men' who subsequently came to be treated as untouchables. Ambedkar considers the roots from which *untouchability* has sprung is, the contempt and hatred of 'broken men' as of Buddhists by Brahmins and the continuation of beef eating by these 'broken men' after it was given up by others. Most of the scholars identified the untouchability with impure.

Ambedkar felt that this is an error and *untouchables* are distinct from the impure. While the impure as a class came into existence at the time of *Dharma Sutra*, the untouchables came into being much later than 400 A.D. Historically, Ambedkar connects untouchability with 'cow killing' for which capital punishment was given during the Gupta period in 400 A.D. The beef eating sudras were made not only impure but untouchables. Ambedkar came to a conclusion that, 'we can therefore say with some confidence that untouchability was born some time about 400 A.D. It is born out of the struggle for supremacy between *Buddhism* and *Brahminsm* which completely moulded the history of India and the study of which is so woefully neglected by the students of Indian history.[34]

Ambedkar identified four fundamental rules of *caste*. A *caste* may be defined as a social group having belief in Hindu religion and bound by certain regulations as to marriage, food and occupation. There can be no inter-marriage between different castes. This is the first and the most fundamental idea on which the whole fabric of caste is built up. In the matter of food the rule is that a person cannot take food from and dine with any person who does not belong to his caste. This means those who can intermarry can also interdine. Those who cannot intermarry cannot interdine. In this way caste is both as endogamous and communal unit.

In the matter of occupation, the regulation is that a person must follow the occupation that is the traditional occupation of his caste and if the caste has no occupation then he should follow the occupation of his father. In the matter of status of a person, it is fixed is hereditary. It is fixed because a person's status is determined by the status of the caste to which he belongs. In a social group individual person becomes a member without any act of volition, and becomes subject to social regulation and traditions over which he has no control of any kind. *Caste* has been given name. It is in the name that the *caste* bears which gives it fixity, continuity and individuality. There is no interconn-ection between various castes, which form a system. And each caste is separate and distinct. It is independent and sovereign in the disposal of its internal affairs and enforcement of caste regulations. The caste relates to other in the order of vertical and not horizontal.

Ambedkar identified some of the features of caste system as hierarchy, lack of social efficiency, social immobility, disruptive tendencies, ex-communication, endogamy and anti-social spirit. The effects of this system are that it prevents assimilation, creates indifference and makes the Hindus inactive. It creates obstacles for any reforms and leads to economic and social backwardness. Ultimately both social and natural justic is denied for lower castes.

Ambedkar considered that there is no doubt that caste system is an evolution of the *varna* system. One may not get any idea of caste system by studying *varna* system. He argues that caste must be studied apart from *varna* and it is a perversion of *varna.*

Each *caste* is separate and distinct. It is independent and sovereign in the disposal of its internal affairs and the enforcement of caste regulations. The castes touch but they do not interpenetrate. One caste stands in relation to other castes in the system. That order is vertical and not horizontal. To follow the workings of *caste* in action it is necessary to note another feature of caste besides the *caste* system, namely, class-caste system. Ambedkar too brings the debate of *caste* and class. Some were of the opinion that caste is analogous to class and that there is no difference between the two. Others hold that the idea of castes is fundamentally opposed to that of class. Ambedkar noticed that although caste is different from and opposed to the notion of class yet the caste system—as distinguished from caste—recognises a class system, which is somewhat different from the graded status, referred to above. He illustrates this point through the example. Just as the Hindus are divided into so many castes, castes too are divided into different classes of castes. The Hindu is caste-conscious. He is also class-conscious. Whether he is caste-conscious, or class-conscious depends upon the *caste* with which he comes in conflict. If the caste with which he comes in conflict in a caste within the class to which he belongs he is caste-conscious. If the caste is outside the class to which he belongs he is class-conscious. It is evident from the study of *Non-Brahmin movement* in Madras and Bombay presidency.[35]

Caste as an Anti-Social Principle

Hindu society is nothing but a collection of castes. Each caste is conscious of its existence and caste has no feeling that it is affiliated to other caste except there is a Hindu-Muslim riot. Each caste not only dines among itself and marries among itself but each caste prescribes its own distinctive dress.

Men constitute a society because they have things, which they possess in common. To have similar things is totally different from possessing things in common. Making the individual a shareholder, or partner in associated activity allows for the feeling of belongingness, its failure results in a glueless society. There is nothing to bind people together. The *caste system* prevents common activity and by preventing common activity it has prevented the Hindus from becoming a society with a unified life and a consciousness of its own being.

Caste has destroyed the sense of public charity. *Caste* killed public spirit. Virtue has become caste-ridden and *morality* has become caste-bound. There is no sympathy to the deserving. There is no appreciation for merit. There is no charity to the needy. There is charity but it begins with caste and ends with the caste. There is sympathy but not for the men of other castes.

It is argued by some thinkers that caste is an evolution of *varna* system. Ambedkar argues that caste is the perversion of *varna*. At any rate, it is an evolution in the opposite direction. But while caste has completely perverted the *varna* system it has barrowed the class system from the *varna* system. Indeed the class-caste system follows closely the class cleavages of the Varna system. *Chaturvarna* system brings the cleavages in society. It keeps one social group above another group. In a pyramid of caste hierarchy, Brahmins, Kshatriyas, Vaishyas are placed in the higher order and Sudras below.

According to the classical *varna system*, while Brahmins were the literati, Kshatriyas were martial and Vaishyas practised trade and Sudras were the labouring classes. The first three classes were treated as regenerate classes, whereas the latter, sudra, was held as unregenerate class. The customs in all their strictness were obtainable only in one caste, namely the Brahmins, who occupied the highest place in the social hierarchy of the Hindu society. Their prevalence in the non-Brahmin castes is derivative of whether their observance is strict, or complete. The priestly class were considered to be the originators of this unnatural institution. It was founded and maintained through quite unnatural means. The caste rules were codified and philosophized by Manu. Apart from these four *varna* groups, there were certain people/ social groups living outside the *chaturvarna*. They were known as *avarnas*.

The working of the *caste system* was not purely functional. It not just divided the people but humiliated some groups and legitimised this division through religious texts. The *caste system* is not merely a division of labour, but a division of labourers. It is a hierarchy in which the division of labourers are graded one above the other. The peculiar character that prevails in India is that the division of labour accompanies gradation of labourers. This division of labour is not based on natural aptitudes. This division brought by *caste system* is compelled, not based on individual choice. Individual sentiment and individual preference has no place in it. It is based on the dogma of predestination. As an economic organisation caste is a harmful institution, as it involves the subordination of man's natural powers and inclinations to the exigencies of social rules.

Ambedkar made an attempt to interpret Indian society by using Marxian methodology for his own convenience. Contrary to the opinion of ancient India does not have any history, Ambedkar tried to dig out its history with the help of Buddhist literature. The rise of *Buddhism* in ancient Indian society was considered by him as a revolution against Aryan Brahminism. More than religious revolution, it is social and political. The Brahmins became the custodians of religion by monopolising the priestly profession. This gave them scriptural authority to guide the people in all its moral and spiritual matters. They set the standards for others. The Aryan community at the time of Buddha was steeped in the worst kind of debauchery: social, religious and spiritual. The Aryan religion never concerned itself with what might be called a righteous life. In the Aryan society, the sudra/low caste man could never become a Brahmin. But Buddha not only preached against caste but also admitted them at the rank of *bhikku*. The decline of *Buddhism* followed the triumph of *Brahmanism*. This, Ambedkar considered as counter-revolution. Further, this counter-revolution lead to the downfall of the sudras and women. He finds the riddles of Hinduism in its sacred literature. He questioned the very authority of Vedic literature and its privilege of *apaurusheya*.

Ambedkar's Conception of Religion

Ambedkar's social and *political philosophy* centred around his conceptions about religion. He tried to construct community on the foundations of religion. His idea of religion is philosophical and more rooted in normative behaviour. He stressed more on the philosophy of religion rather than religiosity. He regards it as both descriptive and normative. He considers that in so far as it deals with the teachings of religion, the philosophy of religion becomes descriptive. In so far as it involves the usage of critical reason for passing judgment on those teachings, the philosophy of religion becomes normative. Based on the normative judgments, he negated *Hinduism* as a religion that doesn't stand to be a religion. Ambedkar argued that philosophy of religion should be based on two norms—social utility and justice for the individual. To be a religion it should pass this test. Ambedkar's judgment would be that Hindu philosophy served neither social utility, nor justice for the individual. He showed that social and religious inequalities were deep rooted in *Hinduism*.

To put forward his conception of religion, he tries to discuss elaborately about the evolution and the meaning of religion. He cautions the readers to be clear about the usage and context of religion since the meaning of the term religion varies from time to time. He considers that the study of philosophy of religion involves:

1. The meaning and understanding of religion,
2. To know the scheme for which a religion stands for; and
3. The criteria to be adopted for judging the value of ideal scheme of divine governance for which a given religion stands for.

Ambedkar judged the philosophy of religion in terms of its capacity to generate revolutions. In simple terms, he thought reason and critical analysis as a method used for the study of religion. In order to explain the religion of modern times, he brings the evolution of religion in his writings. The primitive religion is identified with magic. In the second stage, religion came to be identified with beliefs, rituals, ceremonies, prayers and sacrifices. This period considered beliefs, rites, ceremonies and sacrifices were necessary both to proprate a benevolent power and also to conciliate an angry power. Later, that power was called God, or creator. Following this, the idea of God who created this world and also man got strengthened. The third stage was followed by the belief that man has a soul and the soul is eternal and is answerable to God for man's actions in the world.

There was a time, religion had covered the whole field of knowledge and claimed infallibility for what it thought. The scientific discoveries undermine the religion to an extent. The Copernican revolution freed astronomy from the domain of religion. Darwin's evolutionary theory freed biology and geology from the *trammels* of religion. Ambedkar points out, the disruption of the empire of religion should be treated as a great revolution. He puts more emphasis on the change of religion from the normative point of view. He tries to find out the change of value system from the religion of savage society to the religion of modern civilised society.

Ambedkar observes that in the savage society, there was no trace of the idea of God. There is no bond between morality and religion. There is a religion that exists without God. There is a morality that exists but it is independent of religion. The religion of civilised society differs from that of savage society. In civilised society, God comes in the scheme of religion. *Morality* becomes sanctified by religion. It had undergone further changes which have revolutionised the meaning and moral significance.

The civilised society splits into antique society and modern society. The conception regarding the relationship between god, society and man, too, varies in these forms of societies. Here again, Ambedkar tries to explore the real norm for the basis of religion. He considers that norms must enable people to judge what is right and wrong in the conduct of men. Based on this normative criterion he tries to judge religion. As he observed:

"Utility as a criterion was appropriate to the antique world in which society being the end, the moral good was held to be something which had social utility. *Justice* as a criterion became appropriate to the modern world in which individual being the end, the moral good was held to be something which does justice to the individual."[36]

He applied this method to critically interrogate Hinduism. He came to the conclusion that *Hinduism* neither passed the test of social utility, nor the test of individual justice. So *Hinduism* doesn't stand to be a religion of either antique society, or modern society: "The philosophy of Hinduism therefore neither satisfies the test of social utility, nor does it satisfy the test of individual justice."[37]

Hinduism is premised on the principle of inequality. The arresting feature about Hinduism is *caste* system. The important feature of the caste system is that different castes do not stand as a horizontal series. It is a system in which the different castes are placed in a vertical series, one above the other. *Manu* may not be responsible for the creation of caste. But he gave sanctity to *varna*. In the scheme of *Manu*, *Brahmins* placed in higher rank and sudra and Ati-sudras at the lowest rank. 'This system of rank and gradation is simply another way of enunciating the principle of inequality so that it may be truly said that *Hinduism* doesn't recognise *equality*.'[38] This inequality pervades in the very social relationships among the classes at all times in all places and for all purposes. One has to be blind not to observe this. Ambedkar illustrates this point with various examples from scriptural texts: 'Thus in Hinduism you will find both social inequality and religious inequality imbedded in its philosophy.'[39] Ambedkar questions the basic rules of Hinduism from a rationalistic approach. Further, he argues that *Manu* doesn't stop with the non-recognition of human personality and he advocated the deliberate debasement of human personality.

Ambedkar quotes *Laski* from his book, *Liberty in the Modern State*, that liberty is to be accompanied by certain social conditions. In the first place, there should be social *equality* and in the second place there must be economic security, and in the third place there must be knowledge made available to all.[40] Ambedkar applies this to

Hinduism and finds that at first, it denied equality, the very first condition to exercise liberty. It upholds privilege and inequality. Regarding economic security, Hinduism denied freedom of vocation. In the scheme of *Manu*, each man has his vocation preordained for him before he is born. *Hinduism* allows no choice. The occupation being preordained, it has no relation to the individual's capacity, or inclination. It compels people to serve ends chosen by others. Manu tells the Sudra that he is born to serve the higher classes. He exhorts him to make that his ideal'.[41] Thus in *Hinduism*, there is no choice of a vocation. There is no economic independence and there is no economic security.

Hindus believed that there was no knowledge outside the *Vedas*. The Brahmins alone had the right to teach the *Vedas*. But in the case of the sudra, he was not only allowed to study the *Vedas* but also not allowed even to hear it while reciting. This keeps the general masses in ignorance. Considering all these factors, Ambedkar concluded that Hinduism is opposed to the conditions in which liberty can thrive. It is therefore a denial of *liberty*.

Ambedkar explains that philosophy of *Hinduism* is a direct denial of *fraternity*. It teaches not to interdine, not to intermarry, and not to associate. Fraternity is opposite to *individualism*. It is another name for fellow being. Individualism would produce anarchy. It is only fraternity, which prevents it and helps to sustain the moral order among men. Ambedkar quotes *J.S. Mill*, regarding the sentiment of fraternity of fellow feeling as natural. As *J.S. Mill* quoted by Ambedkar, "The social state is at once so natural, so necessary, and so habitual to man, that, except in some unusual circumstances...Society between equals can only exist on understanding that the interests of all are to be regarded equally...And in every age some advance is made towards a state in which it will be impossible to live permanently on other terms with any body."[42]

As a plant grows only where the soil is propitious and the conditions for its growth exists, Ambedkar observed "The fundamental condition for the growth of the sentiment of fraternity is not preaching that we are children of God, or the realisation that one's life is dependent upon others. The condition for the growth of this sentiment of fraternity lies in sharing in the vital process of life. It is sharing in the joys and sorrows of birth, death, marriage and food."[43]

Ambedkar corrects Lord Acton, inequality has grown as a result of historical circumstance. It has never been adopted as creed'. This is not the case with Hinduism as Ambedkar points out, in *Hinduism* inequality is a religious doctrine adopted and conscientiously preached as a sacred dogma. It is an official creed and nobody is ashamed to profess it openly. Inequality for the Hindus is a divinely prescribed way of life as a religious doctrine and as prescribed way of life. It has become incarnate in Hindu society and is shaped and moulded by it in its thoughts and in its doings.

From the point of view of justice, the philosophy of *Hinduism* is inimical to *equality*, antagonistic to *liberty* and opposed to *fraternity*[44] Against *Hinduism*, Ambedkar proposes *Buddhism* as a religion. He equates *Buddhism* with *dhamma.* He argues *dhamma* is different in the ordinary sense of religion. The *dhamma* of Buddha is to some extent analogous to what the European theologians called religion. Ambedkar points outs how *dhamma* is different from religion. Though religion is considered personal and restricts to private life, *dhamma* is social. It is righteousness; it means right relations between man and man in all spheres of life. Society can't do without *dhamma. Dhamma* should be the instrument of governance. Those who want liberty must therefore have *dhamma.* He reasserts that according to Buddha, *dhamma* consists of *prajna* and *karuna.* These two are the corner stones of *dhamma. Prajna* is an understanding. The implication of this is that, it doesn't allow any room for superstition or dogmatism. *Karuna* is love. Without it society can neither live nor grow. In the words of Ambedkar, 'The unique amalgam of *prajna* and *karuna* is the *dhamma* of Buddha.'[45]

Ambedkar brings Buddhist religion as parallel to *Marxism* in his *Budha or Karl Marx.* He highlighted some points from the readings of *Tripitikas*, the Buddhist literature. Religion is necessary for a free society. It must relate to facts of life and not to theories and speculations about God, or soul, or heaven or earth. It is wrong to make God as centre of religion. Man and morality must be central to it. All human beings are equal. Worth and not birth is the measure of man. Every one has right to learn. Learning is necessary for man to live as food is. Learning without character is dangerous. Religion lives in the heart of man and not in *sastras*. Nothing is permanent, or *sanatan*. Everything is subject to change. Being is always becoming. Nothing is infallible. Nothing is binding forever. Everything is subject to inquiry and examination. The private ownership of property brings power to one class and brings sorrow to another. It is necessary for the good society that this sorrow be removed by removing its cause. War is wrong unless it is for truth and justice.[46]

Marx is interested in scientific socialism. For him the purpose of the philosophy is to reconstruct the world and not to explain the origin of the universe. The forces, which shape the course of history, are primarily economic. The society is divided into two classes, owners and workers, and always a class conflict is going on between these two classes. Since workers are exploited by the owners who misappropriate the surplus value which is the result of the workers' labour. This exploitation can be put to end by nationalisation of instruments of production, i.e., abolition of private property. The growing impoverishment of the workers is resulting in a revolutionary spirit among workers and the conversion of the class conflict into a class struggle. Ultimately, the workers are bound to capture the state and establish their rule that he called the dictatorship of proletariat. These factors are irresistible and therefore socialism is inevitable.[47]

Ambedkar has no agreement with the *Marxism* that economic interpretation of history is only explanation of history and proletariat has been progressively pauperised. He compares Buddhism with *Marxism* on certain fundamental points. The language and the timings of Buddha and Marx are different but the meaning is same in so many points. One finds the common agreement between them. The function of philosophy is to reconstruct the world, the conflict of interests exists between classes, private property brings power to one class and sorrow to another through exploitation, it is necessary for a good society that the sorrow be removed by the abolition of private property-all these principles of Marxism compared with the some of the principles of

Buddhism. To prove this, Ambedkar quotes so many passages from Buddhist literature. Buddha's doctrine of *astanga marga recognisneres* that class conflict which is the cause of misery. If for misery one reads exploitation Buddha is not away from Marx. The rules of Budhists bhikshu sangha are the testimony for the abolition of private property.

Ambedkar considers the means adopted by both seems to be different but the end is the same. The misery and unhappiness, which is caused by the misconduct, could be removed through the practice of *panchsila*. Buddha felt the misery and unhappiness in the world as a result of man's inequity towards man. For the removal of man's inequity towards man the Buddha prescribed the noble eight fold path. The doctrine of *nibbana* tells the difficulties in realisation of this eight fold path. The gospel of Buddha enunciated as a result of his enlightenment to end the sorrow and the misery of the world. The means adopted by Buddha were necessary to convert a man by changing his moral disposition to follow the path voluntarily. The means adopted by the communists are violence and dictatorship of proletariat. Ambedkar felt that the differences are about means, but the end is common to both.

Ambedkar made an effort to evaluate the means of both in order to elevate his beliefs and commitments. First of all, he is not preaching absolute non-violence. He agrees, wherever it is necessary it may be used for just cause in inevitable situations. He says Buddha was against violence. But he was also in favor of justice required, for that he permitted the use of force. This is well illustrated in his dialogue with *Simha Senapati* the commander-in-chief of Vaishali. As Buddha replied, '...A man who fights for justice and safety cannot be accused of *ahimsa*. If all the means of maintaining peace have failed then the responsibility for *himsa* falls on him who starts war. One must never surrender to evil powers. War there may be. But it must not be for selfish ends....'[48]

To support his reading of Buddha, Ambedkar brings his teacher *John Dewey* in this regard. *John Dewey* opposes the conception of 'end justifies the means is a morally perverted doctrine'. He countered this by asking what can justify the means if not the ends? It is only the end that can justify the means. Dewey has pointed out that violence is only another name for the use of force and although force must be used for creative purposes. A distinction between use of force as energy and use of force as violence needs to be made. The use of force must be so regulated that it should save as many ends as possible in destroying one evil.

Ambedkar argues that Buddha's *ahimsa* was not as absolute as the *ahimsa* preached by the Mahavira the founder of Jainism. Buddha would have allowed force only as energy. Generally communists preach *ahimsa* as an absolute principle. Ambedkar reminded that Buddha was deadly opposed to this. Buddha would have probably admitted that it is only the end, which would justify the means. Buddha would have said that if the end justified violence, violence was a legitimate means for the end in view. He certainly would not have exempted property owners from force, if force was the only means for that end.[49]

He accused communists that in achieving one valuable end they are destroying other valuable ends. For example, the end of dictatorship of communists is to make revolution permanent. This is a valuable end. But the communists say that in achieving this end they have not destroyed other valuable ends. He further continued, dictatorship is often defined as absence of liberty, or absence of parliamentary government. In parliamentary government you have a duty and a right, the duty to obey the law and right to criticise it. In dictatorship you have only duty to obey but not right to criticise it.

Ambedkar not only elevates the means of *Buddhism* in realising the same ends proposed by the communists. He also argues in favor of government based on moral disposition. In place of communist's dictatorship of proletariat, he proposes parliamentary government. He considers the communist government as a government by force. To legitimise his position he borrowed another *conservative* western thinker Burke. He quoted *Burke* for his point that force cannot be a lasting means. *Burke* in his speech on conciliation with America warns in this regard. He puts the objection to force on the ground that it has only temporary effects and uncertainty associated with it.[50]

As mentioned earlier, Ambedkar heavily invested on moral society and moral governance like Buddha. He elaborates that, when the moral force fails then brutal force takes its place. What the Buddha wanted was that each man should be morally so trained that he may himself become a sentinel for the kingdom of righteousness. He believes that Buddha established *communism* so far as *sangha* was concerned without dictatorship. Buddha's method was to change the mind of man: to alter his disposition. So that whatever man does, he does it voluntarily without the use of force or compulsion. His means to alter the disposition of men was his *dhamma* and the constant preaching of his *dhamma*.

Ambedkar pointed out that communists have negative conception against religion and had shown hatred against it-'opium of the masses'. Ambedkar argues that communists have carried their hatred of Christianity to *Buddhism* without waiting to examine the difference between the two. *Buddhism* is a humanistic religion and man centered. It is not god centered. It does not believe in rituals. *Buddhism* as religion stands for reason. It is rationalistic religion. He further continues that *communists* are weak in explaining what would take place if the state withers away. If it is succeeded by anarchy, there is no use of building the communist state. One cannot withhold state by force. Ambedkar tried to resolve this situation by proposing Buddhist religion and its spiritual values. The only thing that could sustain it after force is withdrawn is religion. The communist's permanent dictatorship has paid no attention to spiritual values. Humanity doesn't only want economic values; it also wants spiritual values to be retained. In this context he brings *Carlyle's* comment on *communists* that political economy is pig economy. Of course, Ambedkar doesn't endorse this in toto since he recognises man needs material comforts. But he believes that human beings must realise both materially and spiritually. In his own words, 'But the communist's philosophy seems to be equally wrong for the aim of their philosophy seems to be fatten pigs as though men are no better than pigs. Man must grow materially as well as spiritually.'[51]

The *French revolution* came with a slogan of *equality*, *liberty* and *fraternity*. But it failed to produce equality. The *Russian revolution* aimed to produce *equality*. Ambedkar argues that in producing equality society cannot afford to sacrifice, *fraternity* or *liberty*. *Equality* will be no value without *fraternity* or liberty. Ambedkar firmly believes that the three can coexist only if one follows the way of Buddha. *Communism* can give one but not all.

Assessment of Ambedkar's Political Philosophy

From 1980s onwards, studies on Ambedkar in the wake of Dalit movement have proliferated. Most of the studies are on *Dalit movement* in general. Almost all the scholars tried to link up the *Dalit movement* to Ambedkar's thought but there are few studies in estimating his philosophy in general and political theory in particular. The studies try to understand him in existing dominant political traditions. They too find difficulties in locating Ambedkar's political thought in existing political traditions.

K.Raghavedra Rao, well-known political scientist made an attempt to caricature social, political and religious philosophy in Sahitya Academy produced a monograph, *Babasaheb Ambedkar (1993)*[52]. He characterised his political thought broadly as liberal. In the liberal tradition, he tries to find out Ambedkar's version of liberalism to suit Indian context. He argues one may find in Ambedkar, a liberalism that has transformed into a version of neo-pluralism in the context of the new liberal theories of modernisation and development. According to this, liberal state is conceptualised as a focal point for bargaining and relationship of exchange between associational groups of which a society is supposed to be made up. It is a shift from individualism towards group-based politics and collectivist goals. *Raghavendra Rao* identifies that Ambedkar seems to be more inclined towards a neo-pluralistic theory of state, and this is astonishing because he took this position as a liberal even before *liberalism* itself took a pluralistic turn, especially after the Second World War and under the impact of American capitalist ideology.[53] Further he argues, however, for Ambedkar this operational notion of state structurally geared to humanistic ideals of liberty, equality and fraternity. His ideal state was one, which all the three values converged under conditions of equilibrium. He is not a dogmatic in this venture. In Ambedkar's version, a liberal democratic state is the political system that can best tackle this issue.[54]

Raghavendra Rao explains how Ambedkar's liberal democratic state came close to Marxian and *Weberian* conceptions and how he differs from these conceptions. The liberal democratic state itself is not an isolated category and it requires an appropriate context of society, culture and religion to become a functioning reality. Ambedkar would argue that state is in fact a superstructure of a more fundamental structure—society. The economy, too, is a superstructure of this fundamental category. It means society is the base and primary, State and economy emerges out of it. He is in favour of normative society. Society rests itself on the foundations of normative order, which is religious order. To argue this way, of course, is to strike the liberal political theory itself at its roots.[55] Liberal theory presupposes a State that is neutral. This is conceptualised in the liberal model, via its character as a legal entity embodying the rule of law, as a significant autonomous entity.

For Ambedkar, as for the Marxists, the State cannot operate independent of society in any significant extent. But while the Marxists foreground society strongly in the economy, Ambedkar evolved a theory of State with culture as its base. This may look like the *Weberian* notion but it is not. This is for the reason that Ambedkar attaches far greater importance to the economic structure of a society than a *Weberian* would. To that extent he is closer to Marx than to Weber. However, it has to be recognised that Ambedkar distances himself from both Marxian and *Weberian* positions in his political theory.[56]

Gail Omvedt assesses his political thought in search of new vision for India. Her interpretations of Ambedkar's ideas as enunciated in a memorial lecture, "Liberty, Equality, Community: Dr. Babasaheb Ambedkar's Vision of a New Social Order"[57], will be discussed here. Ambedkar, like Marx, is against exploitation, but not against development and accumulation. At a social level, he believes in progress in history, and at an individual level he gives legitimation to honest and energetic efforts of 'householders' to work and earn. While he doesn't fit clearly into a historical materialist position, his writings show an evolutionary and 'stagist' view of history. This social evolutionary model differed from the more economically based versions offered by Marx, or more conventional sociologists. History then, does show progress. What plays the basic role in determining social structure and conditioning human actions? This is the great question of sociological and historical materialism versus idealism (pluralism).

Was Ambedkar an idealist because he gave so much importance to the role of religion and ideas in action?

Gail Omvedt finds difficulty in fixing him to a particular political and philosophical position. At the same time she makes an attempt to develop Ambedkar's political thought. She notes that Ambedkar doesn't spend any time developing, or explicitly stating his methodology. She identifies different phases in Ambedkar and also tries to provide a comprehensive and coherent thought of Ambedkar as a whole in the concrete situations of India. She observes that in his early essay on Russell, he projects the economic interpretation of history and at the other end of his life he seems to have moved towards idealism. He argued against the basic theses of Marx that the economic interpretation of history is the only explanation of history. In *Buddha and his Dhamma*, he gives clear priority to 'mind' as a determinant. He recognises mind as the centre of everything. Mind precedes things, dominates them, creates them.... Mind is the chief of all faculties... The first thing to attend to is the culture of the mind. His study of Indian past in religious terms can be seen in his '*Revolution and Counter-Revolution*'. He reads the stages in history as *Brahmanism*, *Buddhism* and *Hinduism*.

Gail Omvedt characterises Ambedkar's view as pluralistic.[58] She considers that Ambedkar has a significant sociological theory though he was not a trained sociologist, or historian. Ambedkar does show a concern for a logical and a scientific method. Though he stresses 'mind' as primary in his final work, the orientation is very much towards the material world.

Ambedkar's philosophy of history is consistent with the pluralistic explanation of history, though not of a purely materialistic one. This would be a *Weberian* position. Even in his rejection of Marx, Ambedkar, who was never one to use words sloppily, rejects the 'economic interpretation' as the 'only explanation.' He never denies the role of material factors and economic impulses as a necessary part of any overall historical and social explanation.[59]

In characterising his political economy, *Gail Omvedt* differentiates three stages of his thought. The first phase is represented by his writings of 1920s in Economics, 'The problem of Rupee and the evolution of provincial finance in British', and other articles have shown him as a liberal economist, though with a significant Keynesian influence. The second phase, that is 1930s, may be characterised as "dual system" theory. This is the period he actively involved in social movements, not only of Dalits, but also of workers and peasants generally. This is the stage when he declared his struggles against '*capitalism*' and '*Brahminism*' (This is like socialist-feminists, fighting against 'capitalism and patriarchy' and Black radicals against '*capitalism* and racism'). In taking Brahmanism and capitalism as the focus of struggle, Ambedkar was inclined to accept a Marxist understanding by adding an appreciation of the role of caste as an autonomous, exploitative and oppressive social structure. He took *Marxism* as a theory to analyse *capitalism* and supplemented it with an analysis of caste focusing on religion and ideology. This period climaxed with the proclamation of the need for '*state socialism*' in his *State and Minorities*. The final stage started with 1950s with rejection of a Marxist approach to economic issues and its inadequacy on social issues. In his essay on *Buddha* or *Karl Marx*, Ambedkar returns to an appreciation of the role of private accumulation of wealth and gives us a reinterpretation of State, market, and community through Buddhist parable. The *sangha* represents the community, the ideal communist society. 'In spite of these shifting phases, there is no doubt that Ambedkar's political-economic philosophy was a form of liberalism. He was an individualist and rationalist, returning always to the basic enlightenment values linked to Indian tradition.'[60]

Further, *Gail Omvedt* elaborates the liberal position of Ambedkar in the light of many shades of liberalism. She considers Ambedkar as representing the 'social liberalism'. According to this, the State will intervene in resolving the contradiction between inherited inequality and human rights. In this sense, it is different from classical and neo-liberalisms.

The *Naxalite Party* CPI (M-L) (Peoples War) locates Ambedkar theoretically as a liberal bourgeoisie reformer[61] in their document 'Caste Problem in India: Our Point of View' (*Bharatdesamlo Kula Samasya-Mana Drukpadham*). Further, it had a critical attitude in understanding, or estimating Ambedkar's philosophy and his politics.

Ambedkar emerged as a strong leader of the emerging Dalit middle class of his time. 'that Dalit middle class however small). His political beliefs and practices reflect this. Being an important Dalit leader, not carried a struggles in the direction to resolve the primary problems that are responsible for exploiting the Dalit collective as a whole, Dalit agricultural coolies, poor peasant and labour class. He never raised the slogan 'land to the tiller', that is going to transform the lives of the people of more than 95 per cent who are living as agricultural coolies and poor peasants. All his other struggles for spiritual and civil rights, demands for reservations in government jobs, and scholarships reflects the aspirations of emerging Dalit middle class rather than Dalits as a whole.

The party considers Ambedkar as Anti-Marxist philosophically. Because of his leanings towards liberal bourgeoisie philosophy, he opposed the Marxist understanding that the social change through revolution and the development through class struggle. He brings non-violent *Buddhism* parallel to Marxism, to counter the Marxian revolution through violence.[62]

The Naxalite party finds problems in fixing his political position. It explains that though essentially Ambedkar is a representative of petty bourgeoisie, his life may be divided into two phases. The first phase is till 1941 and the second phase is after 1941. Till 1941, all his activities are pro-people and played an active role in consolidating and running the peoples' movement. Initially the struggles are for social and civil rights and later it is for the democratic rights of peasants and labourers. He led the movements of anti-caste that are part of anti -feudal struggles. In the latter phase, he served the British imperialists and *Comprador* bourgeoisie and feudal classes by involving in the Viceroy's and *Nehru's* cabinets and drafting committees, he helped forces of anti-democratic forces of his times. He limited his struggles to reform and thus indirectly helped the undemocratic forces. So the Left Party appeals to its party workers to uphold the phase of Ambedkar's involvement with democratic struggles, and at the same time, exposing his role in favouring the ruling classes and its undemocratic ideals towards the latter phase.

The document is marking Ambedkar as an idealist. Philosophically, Ambedkar accepted idealism by rejecting materialism. This ultimately paved the way for him upholding *Buddhism* as an alternative to *Hinduism*. This idealism is reflected in the problem of *Annihilation of Caste*. Under the influence of idealism, he argues that caste came into existence from Hinduism, instead of explaining its origin from the ancient productive relations of India. As a result he believed that reforming Hinduism instead of changing the social system could annihilate caste. He has not realised that without attacking the social and economic foundations, caste could not be annihilated.

The same idealism made him depend on the British political machinery in his struggles against caste hegemony. He thought that the British Government could be against caste Hindu ideology, since they belonged to the religion of Western Christianity. He didn't consider the British as imperialist. He didn't recognise that the intention of British imperialists is to protect caste rather than waging struggles against caste.

The Party believed that the liberal bourgeoisie thinking of Ambedkar led him to a wrong conception of the nature and function of State. By believing the State as a neutral agent, he ignored the class character of the State. He created an illusion among the people that law and constitutional reforms could bring changes in the very nature of State. He is unable to find out the anti-democratic attitude of the bourgeoisie dictatorship. In essence though, he got inspired from the bourgeoisie democratic revolutionary principles like *equality*, *liberty* and *fraternity*. He didn't recognise imperialism and its class character. As a result, he was deeply involved in reformism in bringing out social change by depending on law, judiciary, parliament and constitution. This justifies his position ideologically as a liberal bourgeoisie reformer.[63]

Dr. Anand Teltumbde, a Dalit scholar sympathetic to both the struggles of Dalits and Naxalites, considers Ambedkar as a *radical thinker*. In his monograph, *'Ambedkar' In and for the Post-Ambedkar Dalit Movement*[64] he points out that many students of the *Dalit movement* are influenced by the post-Ambedkar reflections in characterising Ambedkar as a bourgeoisie liberal democrat....The folklore is that 'Ambedkar' needs to be replaced by the radical 'Ambedkar', who would inspire people to claim the whole world as theirs and not to beg for petty favours from robbers.[65]

He made an effort to highlight the radical image of Ambedkar from the very implications of his thought. He considers locating Ambedkar's thought in liberal and Marxist traditions. One has to understand him in a social context he is operating rather fixing him in a particular position. He notes that Ambedkar in his first essay on caste, a Marxist orientation inspired by his supervisor Prof. *Seligman* is visible. In his later works, Ambedkar is more close to the liberal tradition than *Marxism*. However, consciously he never identified himself with *liberalism*. Being aware of its pitfalls, he needed to declare that he was not a liberal reformist, although while having reservations with the postulations of *Marxism* he could never hide his attraction towards him. The influence of *liberalism* on Ambedkar is more pronounced after he accepted the role of the chairman of drafting committee for the Indian *Constitution* in collaboration with *Congress*. Teltumbe explores Ambedkar's thought in the light of failure of the liberal democratic State of India. He felt that liberal *democracy* might appear better than the decadent Hindu *caste system* but it is incapable of bringing any real change in favour of Dalits. It muffles the tension of the exploitative system and kills the revolutionary motivation of its victims.[66] Further, he argues that Ambedkar was misunderstood as a liberal because of upholding the ideals of *equality*, *liberty* and *fraternity*. In fact, he denies that he had adopted them from the French revolution. He said he had derived them from the teachings of Buddha. These principles were the clarion call of the *French revolution* but later became the ideological props of the liberal bourgeoisie in Europe. Since Marx had ridiculed these principles as the fantasy of bourgeoisie society, many people tended to stereotype Ambedkar as a petty-bourgeois *liberal democrat*. According to Ambedkar, the source of these principles is different from the French revolution. So Marx's ridicules don't apply to him and it is substantially different from that associated with the liberal bourgeoisie.

For *Anand Teltumbde* the basis for projecting Ambedkar as a radical is that his philosophy of the annihilation of caste is in the direction of the goal of *liberty*, *equality* and *fraternity*. Ambedkar clearly understood that caste stood on multiple props in Indian society. That is, the religio-cultural relations, feudal relations in the village setting of which land relations constituted the crux and the socio-political nexus with the State. Annihilation of caste thus needed destruction of all of them. He rightly diagnosed that caste system is basically sustained by the peculiar economic constitution of the Indian village of which the land relations was the main feature. This kind of understanding of Indian society is unique to him and no others had identified this in the politics of his times. The Reformists, the *Congress*, Territorial nationalists, *Communists* and the Muslim league who were active in the politics of his time had not bothered to think in this direction.

Ambedkar realised the necessity of political power for the attack on caste system. Even to bring about residual change in the belief system either through the cultural, or religious route, he stressed the necessity of political power. At the same time, in the given time, he was not prepared to confront the State. As an alternative he proposed, feudal relations in the village could be destroyed only if the private ownership of the land is abolished and co-operativisation of farming is introduced. He thought this structural change could be effected through the constitution.

Many thinkers and radical political parties made an attempt to project Ambedkar as a *liberal* thinker. As I have discussed earlier, *liberalism*, a political theory developed in the West has a theoretical basis and reflection of modern industrial capitalist society. It implies individual rights as natural and absolute. Ambedkar seems to reject the liberal notion of society as an aggregation of individuals related to each other as individuals in terms of the goal of promoting individual interest. He has given importance to justice than utility. According to him utility is only a secondary criterion for judging right, or wrong. That is, primacy of justice over utility is axiomatic for him. By subordinating utility to justice in his philosophical analytical scheme, Ambedkar departs from the very first tenet of *utilitarianism* in particular and liberal philosophy in general.

Another question that can be raised is weather Ambedkar is an individualist in his social and *political philosophy*? Does he follow the liberal thought regarding this? The liberal thought maintains that essence of the individual is economic satisfaction, i.e., consumption. For the Marxists (radicals), individual is essentially a producer, and since production is essentially social, the individual evaporates in the realm of social. But for Ambedkar, *individualism* means transcending ones individuality through the exercise of ones capacity for moral responsibility. The locus of moral responsibility is the recognition of an objectively existing moral law, or *dharma*. It is an ideal which Ambedkar considers central to his version of Buddhist religion.

Ambedkar had differences with both *Gandhi* and the Marxian point of view. *Gandhi* attended the problem of untouchability in his own way. *Gandhi* is a nationalist thinker who also worked for the emancipation of Dalits in the name of *Harijans*. *Gandhi* viewed untouchability from a Hindu religious perspective. To him the central problem was how eradication of *untouchability* could be tackled through self-introspection and changing the heart of upper caste Hindus. Gandhian model addressing the oppressed classes within the Hindu society and viewed that one should not make an issue of their problems as separate one from the overall nationalist demand for national independence. In consequence the Gandhian model supports a strategy of internal social reform of Hindu society. He considers the problem of untouchability as the problem of self. He sees the practice of untouchability by *Hinduism*, as a sin against God and man. He proposed the conversion of heart and self-purification. He accepts the *Varnashrama dharma*. He romanticised the rural village. Ambedkar considers caste system as not only a structure of cultural values but also a certain patterns of equitable distribution of power and wealth of different kinds along the lines of caste hierarchy. He gave up the hope of reform of the Hindu religion. Inspired by Ambedkar, Dalit radicals in the 70s retaliated that the heart of caste Hindu was scattered all over—in land, wealth, property, socio-political power. Unless you transform these, it was difficult to effect the conversion of heart of caste Hindu.

Ambedkar viewed the problem of *untouchability* as a political and economic one. For him, untouchability is a product of the caste system upheld by the upper castes. He wanted transformation at a social and structural level to effect a change in caste-biased discrimination. He also highlighted the role of the State in bringing about social change, particularly through legislative measures. Ambedkar's model advocates the acquisition of political power by exploited groups. It is also interesting that both *Gandhi* and Ambedkar overcome tradition-modern dichotomy advocated by the Western colonial intellectuals. For Gandhi, it was by advocating *Hind Swaraj*, but for Ambedkar it was by holding the legacy of *Buddhism*, the indigenous democratic tradition, that stood for reason.

Ambedkar's accepted many of the basic assumptions of *Marxism*. Its most important aspect is the identification of economic exploitation with private property. His understanding of *Marxism* was used in an attempt to formulate a historical theory of caste and social struggle in India. Ambedkar criticised Marxism on the basis of ethicality. He questioned the basic tenets of *Marxism*, that the 'end justifying the means' and 'religion as the opium of the masses'. Ambedkar considers that for both Buddha and Marx the end is common but the only difference is the means that they professed. The means adopted by communists are violence and dictatorship of the proletariat whereas for Buddha, it is love and compassion, conversion of man by changing his moral disposition to follow the path voluntarily. Ambedkar considers Buddha as first revolutionary since he rejected caste system and social inequality and for his idea of *Sangha*. He comments on the issue of religion, that communists have carried the hatred of Christianity to *Buddhism* without waiting to examine the difference between two. Ambedkar also believes that humanity does only want economic values, but also wants spiritual values to be retained. Ambedkar tries to see the similarities between *Buddhism* and Marxism and also differences. Ambedkar argues that in India there is not only division of labour but also division of labourers exists. He also felt that economic interpretation of history is not only the explanation of history. *Buddhism* for Ambedkar stands for reason. In fact, for both Buddha and Marx the ends remain same but the means differ. For Marx, the means are violent takeover of the State through dictatorship of proletariat. For Buddha, it is conversion of man by changing his moral disposition to follow the path voluntarily. Ambedkar put the question to Marxists, what will take place of state when it whether away. He expressed the doubt that the anarchic situation may take place. Ambedkar proposed *Dhamma* in place of it.

Ambedkar developed his own version of socialism. He termed it as state socialism, which emerges from his interpretation of democracy. Ambedkar from the beginning argues that the *communists* failed to understand the genesis of caste system. *Communists* in India treated caste as a form of social oppression. It does not have material base. As far as Dalits were concerned, caste was an instrument of social as well as economic exploitation. The communists failed to recognise caste specific exploitative system of Indian society. Ambedkar very much emphasised that caste is not only the division of labour but also division of laborers in India.

One has to understand the political philosophy of Ambedkar in the context of his life and struggles. For instance, in the initial stages he took the programme of temple entry. Later, he didn't consider *Hinduism* as having the potential for inclusion of Dalits. Also, he experimented with Marxists and organised joint agitational programmes of Marxists. After some time he formed an independent political party for Dalits. All these phases provide an understanding of the enormous dynamism of Ambedkar. It is wrong to consider him as *'liberal bourgeoisie'*, or *'social liberal'*. All this criticism came from a universe alien to Ambedkar and the community for which he was fighting.

Notes

1. Kymlicka, Will, Contemporary Political Philosophy: An Introduction. Oxford: Clarendon Press, 1990, pp. 95-155.
2. Knowles, Dudly: Political Philosophy, London: Routledge, 2001 : 177-237.
3. Gough, J.W., John Locke's Political Philosophy, Oxford: Clarendon Press, 1974.
4. Sabine, George H. A., History of Political Theory, New Delhi: Oxford and IBH Publishing Co., 1973 pp. 608-680.
5. Dallmayr, Fred R., 'Political Theory at Cross Roads' in From Contract to Community, Marcel Dekkar, Inc. New York, 1978, p. 1.

6. *Ibid.*, p. 9.
7. *Ibid.*, p. 9.
8. Bay, Christian, "Thoughts on Liberalism and Post-Industrial Society" in From Contract to Community, pp. 29-45.
9. Roudrigues, Valerian (Ed.), The Essential Writings of B.R. Ambedkar, New Delhi : Oxford University Press, 2002, p. 61.
10. *Ibid.*, p. 62.
11. *Ibid.*, p. 62.
12. *Ibid.*, p. 62.
13. *Ibid.*, p. 62.
14. *Ibid.*, p. 63.
15. *Ibid.*, p. 63.
16. *Ibid.*, p. 64.
17. Ambedkar, B.R., Dr. Babasaheb Ambedkar Writings and Speeches, Vol. 2, Mumbai: Education Department, Government of Maharashtra, 1982, pp. 429-458.
18. Quoted in Vol. 17, part one, p. 68 from Kheer, pp. 114-117, 121-123.
19. Ambedkar, B.R., Dr. Babasaheb Ambedkar Writings and Speeches, Vol.17 (Part-1), Mumbai: Education Department, Government of Maharashtra, p. 75.
20. *Ibid.* p.76.
21. Ambedkar, B.R. Dr. Babasaheb Ambedkar Writings and Speeches, Vol. 9 Mumbai: Education Department, Government of Maharashtra, 1991, p. 12.
22. *Ibid.*, p. 13.
23. *Ibid.*, p. 17.
24. Ambedkar, B.R., Dr. Babasaheb Ambedkar Writings and Speeches, Vol. 1, Mumbai: Education Department, Governement of Maharashtra, 1989, p. 41.
25. *Ibid.*, p. 43.
26. *Ibid.*, p. 45.
27. *Ibid.*, pp. 46-47.
28. *Ibid.*, p. 47.
29. *Ibid.*, p. 51.
30. *Ibid.*, p. 57.

31. *Ibid.*, p. 77.
32. Burke, Edmund, quoted by Ambedkar in Dr. Babasaheb Ambedkar Writings and Speeches, Vol.1 Mumbai: Education Department, Governement of Maharashtra, 1989. p. 76.
33. Bayle, Susan, Caste, Society and Politics in India. Cambridge University Press: Cambridge, 1999. p. 12.
34. B.R. Ambedkar. The Untochables : Who were they and why they became Untouchables, p. 93.
35. Ambedkar, B.R. Dr. Babasaheb Ambedkar Writings and Speeches, Vol. 1. Mumbai: Education Department, Governement of Maharashtra, 1989, p. 146.
36. Ambedkar, B.R. Dr. Babasaheb Ambedkar Writings and Speeches, Vol. 3. Mumbai: Education Department, Government of Maharashtra, 1987. p. 22.
37. *Ibid.*, p. 71.
38. *Ibid.*, p. 25.
39. *Ibid.*, p. 36.
40. *Ibid.*, p. 38.
41. *Ibid.*, p. 39.
42. *Ibid.*, p. 39.
43. *Ibid.*, p. 45.
44. *Ibid.*, p. 64.
45. *Ibid.*, p. 66.
46. Rodrigues, Valerian, Essential writings of B.R. Ambedkar. New Delhi. Oxford University Press, 2002, p. 59.
47. Ambedkar, B.R., Dr. Babasaheb Ambedkar Writings and Speeches, Vol. 3 Mumbai: Education Department, Government of Maharashtra, 1987 p. 442.
48. *Ibid.*, p. 443.
49. *Ibid.*, pp. 450-51.
50. *Ibid.*, p. 451.
51. *Ibid.*, p. 453.
52. *Ibid.*, p. 462.
53. Raghavendra Rao, K, Babasaheb Ambedkar, New Delhi: Sahitya Academy, 1998.
54. *Ibid.*, p. 35.

55. *Ibid.*, p. 35.
56. *Ibid.*, p. 36.
57. *Ibid.*, p. 36.
58. Omvedt, Gail. Liberty, Equality, Community, Dr. Babasaheb Ambedkar's Vision of a New Social Order, 2000, in www.Ambedkar.org/Research.
59. *Ibid.*
60. *Ibid.*
61. *Ibid.*
62. Bharata Desamlo Kula Samasya-Mana Drukpadham (People's War Document), 1996, p. 25.
63. *Ibid.*, p. 24.
64. *Ibid.*, p. 25.
65. Dr. Anand Teltumbde, 'Ambedkar' In and for the Post-Ambedkar Dalit Movement, Pune: Sugawa Prakashan, 1997.
66. *Ibid.*, pp. 40-41.
67. *Ibid.*, p. 48.
68. Sarkar, Sumit "Indian Democracy: The Historical Inheritance," In Atul Kohli (Ed.) The Success of India's Democracy, Cambridge: Cambridge University Press, 2001.

3

Theorising Dalit Movement

General Understanding of Social Movements

Social movements are viewed as institutionalised collective actions, guided by an ideology and supported by an organisational structure. The objectives, ideology, programme, leadership and organisation are the components of any social movement and they are crucial in building up the movement. The movements aim at collective effort to promote, or resist change. The movement mobilises people into collective action and strives towards a new imagination of freedom. The social movements are generally classified into (a) *reform movements,* i.e. seeking modifications within the framework of existing value scheme and attempt to improve the society without greatly changing its basic social structure. (b) *revolutionary movements,* i.e. those that attempt to replace the existing system with a new one and change society through challenging fundamental values and opposing reformers. (c) *resistance, reactionary movements* block change, or seek to reverse to some recent change. These are viewed as counter movements.

From the 1960s and 1970s onwards, the US and Europe saw an upsurge of protests and demonstrations against governments, government policies, and social conventions. The people involved in these protests often cut across class divisions, and the issues involved new demands such as anti-nuclear, anti-armaments, women's movement, and movements which demand that society recognise and accept different lifestyles, such as gays and lesbians. Theorists tried to understand these protests, to situate them in the debate on theory, and to predict their future course.

In the US, early theories focused on grievances and on the irrational reaction of actors as causes of the movement. This was known as the *breakdown theory*. This was soon rejected by scholars of social movements as they tried to show that a lot of these movements did not lack coherence and design and were not a result of irrational reaction as were said to be. This was followed by what became known as the *resource mobilisation theory*. This theory focused not on why the movements take place, but on how the movement is organised, and why some of them were more successful than others. It was called resource mobilisation theory because the theory purported to show that the success of a movement depended on the resources available to be used. These resources arose from inducing individuals to participate and contribute to the cost. Individuals participated because they saw the benefits to be derived from joining. Success also depended on the movement being able to link to other networks of groups and organisations. The resource mobilisation theory's stress was wholly on the *strategy* to make the movement succeed in demanding for a change in government policies or legislation. Thus, it is sometimes said that the theory focused on political action or the realm of politics rather than on civil society.

A variant of the theories, which focuses on the political, rather than the civil society realm is the *political process approach*. This approach sees social movements as a form of mass politics. The social movement is theorised in relation to the State. The chance of the movement achieving success is discussed in terms of the 'opportunities' that are available. If the government is strong and committed to repression, social movements are likely to fail. But if the government is weak, political opportunities may arise which allow the movement to be successful. Those who adopt this political process or political opportunities approach pay less attention to the 'resource' aspects of the movement. They focus wholly on the interaction between the movement and the State and on ways in which the political system frames the failure or success of the movements.

There are many theories in explaining the social movements on why people struggle. The theories are broadly divided into sociological and psychological.

Sociological theories: *Relative deprivation theory*, it holds that one feels deprived according to the gap between expectations and realisations. *Resource mobilisation theory* attributes importance to effective use of resources in promoting social movements. It sees leadership, organisation and tactics as major determinants of success or failure of social movement. It stresses on techniques rather than causes of movement. It ignores the importance of consciousness and the ideological aspects of the participants. It explains protest movements, and movements of revolt, but do not analyse revolutionary movements. Protests do not necessarily lead to a movement. The deprivation theorists view movements as 'temporary aberration' rather than as 'ongoing process of change'.

Psychological theories: These find the roots of social movements in the personalities of the followers. *Discontent theory* holds that movements are rooted in discontent of the followers. There is a view that people may endure great discontent without joining any social movement. Many societies have endured great poverty, inequality, brutality and corruption for centuries without serious social protest. *Personal maladjustment theory* sees social movements as a refuge from personal life. Movements find their supporters among unhappy, frustrated persons whose lives lack meaning and fulfilment. These psychological theories do not deal with the socio-economic structure, which is a source of deprivation. The psychological dimension of participants is important but not sufficient. The theory of relative deprivation is largely confined to the acts of individual revolts. It doesn't explain the nature and reasons for collectivity and collective actions.

Apart from this kind of classification, there is well-influenced theory both in academics and society in general, that is the Marxian theory of revolution. It is much more sociological than psychological. According to this theory, people make their own histories. Human history is nothing but the story of class struggles. It believes that both individual and society are always in a dynamic state and change from one state to another. In the process of development, people who had the control over the resources become privileged and dominate the other. Obviously they enjoy power. They tried to mould the social institutions in favour of them. It is explained by Marx that the people who own the means of production emerged as a dominant and exploitative class/group. History, polity, culture all was tuned accordingly. If we have a look at human history, the people who are sufferers/oppressed or the victims of this exploitation were never quite silent. Human beings cannot be permanently imprisoned in the existing social structure. Nobody can impose moratorium on his/her creativity forever. Well aware of her/his condition in society, with rise of consciousness, s/he struggles against the oppressive structures and exploitation. In other words, whenever any person feels 'scarcity', s/he will definitely struggle against it. As Marx said, men makes their own history, but they don't make it just as they please; they don't make it under circumstances chosen by themselves, but under circumstances directly encountered, given and transmitted from the past. Since human beings are the products of material and social conditions, to change the conditions they have to fight collectively. In the social production which they carry on, they enter into definite relations that are indispensable and independent of their will. These relations of production correspond to a definite stage of development of their material power of production. The sum total of these relations of production constitutes the economic structure of society-the real foundation on which is raised the legal and political superstructures and to which correspond definite forms of social consciousness. The mode of production in material life conditions the general character of the social, political and spiritual process of life. It is not the consciousness of humans that determines their being, but on the contrary, their social being determines their consciousness. At a certain stage of their development, the material forces of production in society come into conflict with the existing relations of production. With the change in the economic foundation the entire immense superstructure is more or less rapidly transformed.

The early theorists came mostly from Marxist traditions of political economy. They were concerned that the Marxist analysis of social movements, which stresses the importance of consciousness, ideology, social struggle and solidarity, seemed inadequate to explain and characterise these new movements. The new movements are about the environment, women and sexual identities. But instead of focusing on strategies and on the requirements of success or failure, the European debate focused on *why these non-class-based movements arose*. They argued that theories which stress the primacy of structural contradictions, economic classes and crisis in determining collective identities are inappropriate to understand movements which did not appear to have a class base, and did not seem to be related to any crisis, or structural contradiction. However, they were not at all impressed by the US theories of resource mobilisation and political process. They asserted that present day collective action is not confined to negotiations and strategic calculations by social movements to gain political power. Rather, the movements involve issues of social norms and identity, and the struggle take place in the realm of civil society rather than in the realm of politics.

The European debate gave rise to what is now called the new social movement theory. *Alain Touraine* and Jurgen Habermas are among the prominent European theorists. There are variations in emphasis, but in general the new social movements' approach explains the social movements as linked to the failure of the democratic system in post-modern society to guarantee individual freedom, *equality* and *fraternity*. In the view of these theorists, *democracy* is degenerating into an authoritarian, technocratic State. The State in turn has become subjugated to market forces. The State's technocracy and the forces of the market thus dominate people. There are no longer workers, but only consumers. The old class of workers has ceased to be a class in production process. Instead, people's main social role has become that of consumers. In this role, they are manipulated entirely by the market.

For *Habermas*, social movements are seen as defensive reactions to defend the public and the private sphere of individuals against the inroads of the State system and market economy. Similarly, Touraine sees participation in social movements as the only way in which the individual can recover liberty. For both *Habermas* and *Touraine*, the main role of social movements is the mobilisation of 'actors' and 'subjects'-their terms to refer to human beings in their full role as free and creative members of a pluralistic society, as opposed to victims, or objects of State and market domination. Social movements involve a process of self-awareness to create human and social identities, which are free of the domination of the technocratic State and the market. But the creation of these identities is part of the process of a social movement, not its ultimate goal. The social movement is a collective form of action to contest the abuses of political and economic power, and to change the political and market institutions in order to produce a better society. The social movement will come into conflict with existing norms and values. It is a struggle for the autonomy of individuals within a civil society, which has been dominated by the technocracy and the market.

The recent social movements look new. Hence theorists try to explain their novelty by reference to major shifts in society and culture. They conclude that the new social movements are concerned with the construction of new social and political identities, which have been denied by the old State system.

Dalit movement is a struggle against deprivation for centuries. It is a struggle for resource mobilisation and share in political power. It is a democratic revolution of classless and casteless society. It is a struggle of assertion of ones own identity. It is an identity struggle towards equality. Some thinkers like *Gail Omvedt* argues that *Dalit movement* is a new social movement since it is not totally class based. The movement, like *Dalit movement* is enlarging the meaning of freedom. As *Manoranjan Mohanty* explains: movements like Dalit and Women's movements have enlarged the content of freedom, and rights of the social revolution. Some have identified these struggles as social and aims at change in civil society. Some have argued that these movements are as much political as the social. Scholars like *Neera Chandoke* notes that these struggles aim to bring basic linkage between the State, nation-building and civil society. By arguing for their search for self-fulfilment, individuals and groups involve in an alteration in power structure (Partha Chatterjee-political society-community versus state).

Indian State and Political Process

British *colonialism* played a significant role in establishing a relatively centralised State and introducing proto-democratic institutions and practices. In its early phase, British colonialism influenced Indian *democracy* and later Indian nationalists played a role in shaping their version of democracy. Indian *democracy* found its roots in adopting full adult franchise, secularism and federalism. Over the fifty years how far has it succeeded in realising these goals decides the fate of Indian democracy. In the late eighties, there was a serious introspection among the scholars regarding this issue. On one hand, was various marginalised social groups confronting the State for their rights. On the other, the nation witnessed the rise of the Hindu nationalist politics and their attempts in building a *Hindu Rashtra*. Perhaps both these social contexts may have compelled the scholars to study the nature and function of Indian democracy. As *Sumit Sarkar* comments; the political debates that preceded the formation of the Indian constitution in the 1940s had two dominant trends. Some Indian leaders argued simultaneously for full adult franchise, real political *equality* for a variety of religious communities, and genuine federalism with some decentralisation of power in having the sovereign State. This implied for real *democracy*. On the other hand there is a dissent to this position, marked by silences on issues of adult suffrage, overtones of pro-Hindu religious politics and preferences for a unitary, centralised State.[1]

However after independence, the nationalist elite managed to have an Indian State with *democracy*, *secularism* and adult franchise as its ideals and further played a crucial role by bringing diverse social groups under one umbrella in the name of 'unity in diversity'. As a natural inheritance of freedom movement, the *Congress party* took over the State under the leadership of *Nehru*. The *Congress* and its nationalist elites were drawn from often-upper caste and land owning sections of society. The *Congress party* was presided over by the hegemony of a small, upper caste, english-educated elite in collaboration with the regional social elites belonging, by and large, to the upwardly mobile castes of landed peasants. Nehru and his associates employed the rhetoric of socialism, but the political practice was considerably more *conservative*. This is the stage the institutions and practices of democracy found considerable acceptance. There was still no visible opposition or conflict between the rival elites of the Congress. The elite versus mass conflict was also minimal.

Mobilisation of the lower caste was at its infancy and was limited to a few southern states. For about two decades after independence, the left-radical parties and liberal intellectuals, dominated the political discourse on caste. But, this debate was conducted in terms of economic classes alone. The *Congress party* being politically aware of the change in the agrarian context saw castes as socio-economic entities seeking new identities through politics in place of their old identities derived from their traditional status in the ritual hierarchy. Thus, by relying on the caste calculus for its electoral politics and, at the same time, articulating political issues in terms of economic development and national integration, the congress was able to evolve durable electoral bases across castes and to maintain its image as the only truly national party. Its politics was largely addressed to vertically linking the rule of the newly emergent upper castes and English speaking 'national elite' to lower-caste support. The ideology used for legitimating this vertical social linkage in politics was neither class ideology nor caste ideology; the key concept was 'nation-building'.[2]

The modernisation process carried under the State worked out negatively for the lower castes of peasants, artisans, *untouchables* and tribals. Their low status in the traditional hierarchy worked negatively for their entry in the modern sector. Whatever social capital and economic security they had in the traditional status system was wiped out through modernisation process. They remained at the bottom rung of both hierarchies, the sacred and *secular*, caste and class.[3]

By the middle of 1960s, India was caught up in a crisis -both economically and politically. In several northern states the Congress lost heavily as the dissatisfied peasants and middle castes turned to opposition. Almost all the social groups and political forces were in a crisis. Dalits too were affected by the crisis in many ways. As rural agricultural labourers and poor peasants, they suffered both from overall rural poverty and backwardness. They also suffered from the *Nehruvian* model of heavy industries, big dams, over centralised industrial development etc. The economic and social tensions between the landowning middle and upper caste and the lower caste rural poor increased. Those who benefited from agrarian development, a small minority, held the rural political power and influenced the villages. The large majority of middle castes and backward communities were as much victims of the system as Dalits. However the Dalits were at the receiving end of most of the attacks, confronting aggressive backlashes whenever they tried to move ahead. The atrocities committed in practice by a wide range of caste groups, from traditional upper caste elites like Thakurs, Bhumihars and Brahmins to middle castes and lower middle castes like Kunbi-Marathas, Kurmis, Yadavas, Dhangars and Vanniyars are innumerable.

After 1967 congress had, in a sense given up its middle-caste peasants base (especially in north) to the opposition, with the compensation of having strong support among the 'rural poor' and 'the weaker sections', 'harijans, adivasis, Muslims and women'. Even though congress village leaders usually represented the direct exploiters of those sections, they did so in many cases with enough concessions to maintain their power. The Dalit-OBC split was thus replicated in a Congress-opposition political polarisation with the *Congress* drawing its main support base from Dalits and others, while the Socialists and the right-wing opposition sought OBC support.[4]

The next phase from 1970s and 80s has seen the threat to the hegemony of the Congress rule with the emergence of a new generation of mobile citizens. This is a turbulent and uncertain period for many Indians. Many social groups became disillusioned with the Nehruvian Socialism in practice. The political situation is now ripe for democratic changes. To counter the democratic aspirations of various emergent new social groups, the Indian State, under the *Congress*, acquired quite an undemocratic character at this stage. This phase is dominated by rule of *Indira Gandhi*. She too maintained the traditional Congress rhetoric—glorification of the strong, centralised nation combined with semi-socialistic appeals to the poor and the marginalised. The Congress, as a structure of elite patronage, was beginning to crumble. In place of it, the structure of personal loyalty emerged. This situation forced her some reforms and some co-option of representatives of the lower-caste groups along with the already existing powerbase of the local oligarchs. Normless repression, efforts at cooption, political and economic crisis, all intensified in the 1972 to 1975 period in spite of impressive *Congress* victories in the preceding elections. Even while she failed to deliver on her promises to the poor, *Indira Gandhi* broadened the scope of Indian *democracy* towards a greater inclusion of the lower strata.

This is the period where agricultural labourers, peasants, workers and the frustrated middle class were all on move. People started organising against the State and there were struggles all over India in different forms.The Naxalite movement in West Bengal, Bihar, Andhra Pradesh, the Dalit Panthers Movement in Maharashtra, the Chipko movement in the Himalayan region, and organisations like Jharkhand Mukti Morcha, All Assam Students Union, Self Employed Women's Association (SEWA), Tamil Nadu Agriculturalist Association, Khedut Samaj of Gujarat and many other such organisations were all formed during this time.

This period, with the unrest and political mobilisation of various groups, the Left hoped that 'class-like' politics would become true class politics—that broad worker-peasant front under proper party leadership would emerge out of the tradition-bound and caste-defined society of rural India to move toward a revolutionary democratic/socialist transformation. This did not happen.

After Emergency, Janata Party has came to power for a short while. It proved to be only another episode in the ongoing crisis of the ruling elite. The anti-caste oriented Socialists and Brahmin dominated Jana Sangh sections of the party clashed in many areas and the government collapsed.

Emergence of Identity Politics

The period of 1980s marked the beginning of a new era of identity politics. This is the period in which new fundamentalist and ethnic forces were rising on a world scale, in which the forces of liberation were taking disturbing garb. The period from 1990, has seen a new phase in Indian politics. With the decline of the *Congress* hegemony, many experiments were taking place. The decline of the *Congress* has been met by two important developments: the rise of the Bharatiya Janata Party (BJP) especially in the Hindi-speaking areas of the north-central and western India and the growing significance of regional parties, especially in southern India, but also in such other peripheral states as West Bengal, Punjab, and Kashmir. A variety of regional parties have thus become quite significant over the last decade or two. Since many of these parties arose in opposition to the Congress, they often built their power base around intermediate castes-the so-called backward castes in India, which the *Congress* had failed to incorporate.

Democracy ensures formal-legal and not socio-economic *equality.* The growing adoption of the rhetoric of citizenship rights by common Indians has, over time, given rise to numerous demands for more power and resources. Democratic institutions both facilitate such demands and are challenged by them. The impact of democracy and how does it mean to diverse social groups is still a question to be debated. The last two decades shows that Indian masses are dissatisfied with the system. The Indian State has not fulfilled with the promises of equality, secularism and alleviation of poverty. The dissatisfaction of the masses has found diverse expression over the last two decades that often vary from region to region. In the southern states of Tamil Nadu and Andhra Pradesh, the mobilised but unincorporated poor, provide ready support to movie stars-turned-politicians who combine personal and populist appeals to garner popular support. In other states, such as West Bengal and Kerala, reform oriented Communist parties have more systematically incorporated the poor. Where as caste inequalities were deeply rooted-as in the Hindi heartland states-the political emergence of the lowest groups has brought forth new forms of lower-caste politics, either spawning new caste-oriented political parties that cater exclusively to such groups as in Uttar Pradesh, or precipitating violent reactions from threatened higher castes as in Bihar.

Along with the poor, the middling groups of rural Indian society have also become politically active over last two decades. Especially the backward castes came to the forefront with Mandal politics in the centre stage of Indian politics. Also, other middle level rural groups, e.g., the farmers, mobilised for and demanded higher prices for agricultural products and for State subsidies. They alleged that the State was favouring the urban upper classes while neglecting them.

There are many social movements which were witnessed in the last two decades apart from the politics of class and caste. The contemporary social movements mobilised primarily around identity politics like-caste, language and religion. Some others are pursuing specific issues and interests like environmental issues and anti-globalisation struggles. It is a strong conception that social movements strengthen the Indian democracy.

Anti-Caste Movements

In post-independenstet India, the *Dalit movement* is one of the most important social movements, which is fundamentally questioning the perceptions and paradigms of social reconstruction. The *Dalit movement* is an attempt to end the Hindu traditional order and seeks to re-make the world into a new world order. It aims at self-respect and dignity of human beings and social transformation. Its struggle is against the upper caste hegemony and is for a casteless society. Concerning the Dalit movement, Dr. B.R. Ambedkar's philosophy is the source and inspiration. Ambedkar played an influential role on Dalit movement both as an ideological thinker and a political activist.

Before Ambedkar, there were anti-caste struggles in most parts of India in different forms. In the 19th century, social movements and religious symbolism sought to question the foundation of caste system. During this period, one can see many indigenous *yogis* from lower castes questioning the dominance of the upper castes, in the guise of religious movements. They remain limited at the level of spiritual transformation. They didn't see or present the caste problem as political. They were unable to influence the historical events in any significant way. In following days, *Phule* in *Maharashtra, Periyar* in Tamil Nadu, *Narayana Guru* in Kerala and *Ravidas* in Punjab influenced the anti-caste movements in a significant way. Phule proposed the non-Aryan theory, initiated anti-Congress stand and sought for the alliance of the *Shudra and ati-shudras* against Brahmins. *Periyar* led the self-respect movement. He questioned the supremacy of Brahmins by applying the principles of rationalism and followed the atheistic path. *Narayana Guru* proposed, *one caste and one religion*, Ravidas preached the *adi dharma*.

Ambedkar not only learned from the earlier struggles and also realised the limitations of earlier struggles. He read about the *non-Brahmin movement* of Tamil Nadu as it had chosen to fight hegemony of superior castes through gradualist and constitutional methods. He saw that it drew its leadership from middle castes and landed gentry and that went against its spirit and therefore, he realised that it was trapped in imitating the ideals of the Brahmins. Consequently, the struggles become weakened. It is very well evident in the unsuccessfulness of Justice Party in 1944.

Essentially Ambedkar's philosophy is based on two principles, that is, ethical and religious. As he himself claims that his philosophy has roots in religion not in political science. His attack on *Hinduism* is mainly ethical. He felt that Hindu ethics remains at the level of custom and its idea of virtue and sin don't go beyond observance and violation of scriptural injunctions pertaining to rituals and caste practices.

Religion has a central place in his philosophy. To him, the aim of religion is to make a social order in which men abide by a moral code. He considers religion as a social force. He believes philosophers of religion had to be judges by applying the test of justice and test of utility. He considers *Hinduism* as anti religious and *Buddhism* the only religion. It is *Buddhism* that inspired him a lot.

Dalits in the Colonial Period

The word Dalit is a political category in modern times. The people connoted by the term 'Dalit' have a long history with a new term to connote them at every political historical change. Prior to the existence of the term Dalit, these people were identified/named with terms like Avarna, 'Panchama', '*Depressed class*' (1931 census), 'Backward community', '*Untouchable*', 'Harijan', 'Scheduled caste/tribe', 'Adi-Andhra', 'Adi-Hindu', 'Adi-Dravida', 'out castes' etc. There are so many castes that are identified with the word Dalit. Some of these castes are Mahars, Chamras, Bhangi, Mangs, Dom, Paswan, and Valmiki in north India, Mala, Madiga and Relli in Andhra Pradesh, Pallars and Pariahs in Tamil Nadu, Pulayas in Kerala etc., Untouchable identity carried within it both discrimination and resistance. There is a lot of heterogeneity prevailing among the Dalit communities in terms of cultural and linguistic forms. At the same time, there are efforts or conscious attempts to bring these communities together as a unified political and social identity. The struggles of the untouchables are there from time immemorial with different forms. They adopted different strategies with changing social and economic conditions. It seems that sometimes in history, untouchable resistance does not take strict organised form but consists in what James Scott has called the everyday resistance of the weak.[5]

From the moment British rulers began to count Indians, they began inventing criteria to classify and delineate the multiple religions, castes and tribes by an effort of census works of the *British rulers* from 1871 to 1941. The untouchable communities had never seen by the British census officials as an ordinary Hindu of particular caste. Nor were they viewed as a single entity with any internal coherence. The terms used to fix their status were primarily plural and adjectival: they were the *depressed classes*, inferior castes, menial castes, excommunicated castes and so on.[6] One of the early effects of emphasizing the degraded condition of the huge population of 'depressed classes' was to bolster high-caste fears about Hindu vulnerability to Muslim and Christian conversion activities.

Even academics have seen the change of terminology. As *Eleanor Zelloit*, scholar on Dalit studies puts a title for her book on Dalit movement '*From Untouchable to Dalit*' (1994), and an another scholar *Jayashree Ghokhale* who studied the politics of Indian untouchable community puts the title for her book, '*From Concession to Confrontation*' (1993). *Gail Omvedt* puts the title for her book 'Dalits and Democratic Revolution' (1994) for her study on Ambedkar and *Dalit movement* in colonial India. All these inform the direction and politics of the struggles of the Dalits. From the decade of nineties onwards, there is a serious debate raised about caste in academic circles and a considerable amount of literature is produced around the word Dalit and their struggles.

There are considerable studies on Dalits of different parts of the country and on different aspects. *Mark Juergensmeyer* considers caste from cultural-ideological point of view. His study is a detailed examination of how alternative religious vision is developed among the Punjabi untouchables; religion is the medium through which an ideology of social change is constructed. *Juergensmeyer* is sensitive to the secular disabilities suffered by untouchables and his study also brings out some political aspects of Adi-Dharma Movement.[7]

Owen Lynch studied the political development of the untouchable Jatavas. He felt that in India, the caste system is manifested in its own unique cultural idiom, that is, in terms of ritual pollution. He made a point that through the political participation, the Jatavas attempted upward mobility. Political participation leads to the dilution of caste identity and the weakening of the caste organiation, which will gradually make caste a residual problem soluble through changes in consciousness and ideology.

Eleanor Zelloit's work on Ambedkar and Mahars of Maharashtra emphasises the process whereby the Mahars have rejected traditional belief systems and adopted new ideologies. She has examined the motivational and psychological dimensions of change among the Mahars and has hronicled the development of the Buddhist movement with much subtlety from these perspectives. *Gail Omvedt*'s *Dalits and Democratic Revolution* is a study on Ambedkar and the *Dalit movement* in colonial India. It focuses on a materialistic analysis of the origin and development of caste. This compiled the study of Dalit movements in Maharashtra, Tamil Nadu, Karnataka and Andhra Pradesh in pre-independent India. She interprets this from historical materialistic point of view. In pre independent India, there were anti-caste movements in the regions of Tamil Nadu, Maharashtra and Kerala under the leadership of *E.V. Ramaswamy Periyar, Jyothibha Phule* and *Narayana Guru* respectively. Dalits too organised in various forms all over India. Some of the prominent struggles of Dalits are, Adi-Dharma movement of Ravidas in Punjab, Adi-Hindu movement in Western U.P., Nama Sudra movement in Bengal, Adi-Andhra movement in Andhra, Adi-Hindu movement in Hyderabad, Adi-Dravida movement in Tamil Nadu, Adi-Kannada movement in Karnataka. Dalit movement under the leadership of Ambedkar started in Maharashtra in earlier days. Within no time Ambedkar got the imagination of Dalits of all over India in pre and post-independent India.

Ambedkar and the Dalit Movement

Ambedkar was not only the source and inspiration for the *Dalit movement* today; he himself organised many struggles in his lifetime. He emerged from an intellectual and spokesperson of the untouchable

Mahar community of Bombay presidency to an all-India depressed classes leader. The decade of 1920s in Bombay presidency saw the emergence of Dalit movement under the leadership of Ambedkar. This movement drew the people from Mahar community. This movement rejected any idea of pro-Hindu integrationist approach and tried to maintain Dalit autonomy and went on alliance with the forces of non-Brahmin movement. It was concerned about Dalits as workers and peasants by gaining jobs and land.

The great Mahad satyagraha under the leadership of Ambedkar was a remarkable social struggle for the rights of equality of Dalits. It is the declaration of "*untouchables*" in the public sphere for their right to live as full human beings. It is the struggle against Hindu hierarchy and demands the construction of a humane and democratic society. In pre-independent period, especially from 1920s onwards, the Mahars had began to move in a political direction and later established their own political organisation and struggled for primacy of politics in all possible ways. Ambedkar, on behalf of Bahiskrit Hitakarini Sabha submitted a memorandum to Simon commission concerning safeguards for the protection of the interests of the depressed classes as a minority in the Bombay presidency. At the time of the second round table conference (1931), Ambedkar got a lot of prominence at the national level and challenged the position of *Gandhi* in relation to separate electorate for *untouchables* in British India. By that time, Muslims, Sikhs and other communities had already been awarded communal electorate. In the same logic, Ambedkar argued, untouchables were also to be seen as separate, distinct and segregated from the rest of the society. He tried to convince that they should also be extended the same privileges. A severe conflict was brewing between him and Gandhi on this issue. Gandhi blatantly refused to accept a separate political identity for any minority other than Muslims and Sikhs. Ambedkar faced criticism from many sides. *Gandhi* and *Congress* portrayed him as anti-national and pro-British. Attempts were made to depict him as a leader of Mahars and his political movement as a caste movement of Mahars. Congress tried to limit him as a Mahar leader but not as leader of all *untouchable* communities. On the other hand, he was opposed the leaders of other untouchable communities supported by the Congress and the *Hindu Mahasabha*. *M.C. Raja*, the untouchable leader from Madras and Chairman of Depressed India Association, opposed Ambedkar's idea of separate electorates for untouchables and called for a joint electorate with reserved seats for untouchables. He argued that separate electorate would alienate *untouchables* from the larger Hindu society and the untouchables were vulnerable to the reprisals from caste Hindus. His position was very much supported by *Hindu Mahasabha*. (Today's BJP owes its origin to this organisation). The other untouchable community like Chamars too opposed the Ambedkar's idea and his Mahar community.

Chamars, as a community, were less willing to conflict with Hindu society and more willing to work within the Hindu social order in achieving their goals. Their leaders opposed the possibility of the untouchable leaving Hinduism. *Congress* wooing of the Chambhars was done through the action of Chambhar leaders been given seats on Congress tickets in the 1936-37 elections. However, in 1932, the British Government issued communal award and recognised *depressed classes* as a minority community distinct from the caste Hindus and on their basis were given separate electorate as well as the right to vote in general elections They were also given reserved seats in legislative councils. *Gandhi* vehemently opposed this on the ground that it would further the divisions in Hinduism. He went on for an indefinite hunger strike. This ends with the Poona pact of 1932, between *Gandhi* and Ambedkar.

Ambedkar felt the necessity for an independent party of workers and peasants that would fight against both *Brahminism* and *capitalism*. This idea gave birth to the *Independent Labour Party* (ILP from now on) in 15th August, 1936. Most of his speeches and activities centred around socio-religious issues. He cancelled his speech "Annihilation of Caste" and his analysis of the failures of Nasik temple entry Satyagraha are products of this time. This is the period (1936-42) that Ambedkar, and Dalits in general, were caught up in waves of economic and political radicalism. ILP, which condemned the capitalist and landlord injustices, was electorally successful. The general scene all over India was that the newly asserting political forces emphasised the needs of peasants, workers and low castes as central to any real anti-imperialist struggle. They threw a challenge to the Congress party. Later (1942-56), Ambedkar shifted to exclusively organise the Dalits at an all India level in the name of *Scheduled Caste Federation*. Before his death in 1956, he converted into Buddhism along with thousands of his followers.

In post-independent India, there were numerous organisations of employees, youth and students, and political parties in the name of Ambedkar. As *Gopal Guru* explains the category-Dalit is historically arrived at, sociologically presented and discursively presented. We have different categories representing multiple identities in the context of Dalits. The category has not yet assumed any explicit character, and hence, has not closed its linkages with other categories, which also describe reality at different levels and are therefore real. The deployment of Dalit category has logical insight, which contains an element of negation and also conjunction of categories from the same logical class.[8]

Note

1. Seth, D.L, 'Caste and Secularisation Process in India.' In Peter Ronald DeSouza (Ed.) Contemporary India Transitions. New Delhi: Sage Publications, 2000, p. 250.
2. *Ibid,*
3. *Ibid*, p. 252.
4. Omvedt, Gail. Reinventing Revolution: New Social Movements and the Socialist Tradition in India, New York: An East Gate book M.E. Sharpe, 1993.
5. James Scott, Weapons of the Weak: Everyday Forms of Peasant Resistance. New Haven: Yale University, 1985, pp. 28-48.
6. Oliver Mendelsohn and Marka Vicziany, The Untouchables: Subordination, Poverty and the State in Modern India, Cambridge: Cambridge University Press, 1998, p. 71.
7. Juergensmayer, Mark, Religion as Social Vision; The Movement against Untouchability in 20th Century Punjab, Berkely: California University Press, 1982.
8. Guru, Gopal, In Ghansham Shah (Ed.) "The language of Dalit Bahujan Discourse", Dalit Identity and Politics, New Delhi: Sage, 2001.

4

Problems and Philosophical Underpinnings of the Contemporary Dalit Movement

This chapter aims to make sense of the nature of the Dalit movement and to relate the post-Ambedkar *Dalit movement* to the philosophical and political issues discussed by Ambedkar. The precise challenge lies in narrating a story of the Dalit movement. Dalit assertions have been narrated variously by different theories. Dalit assertion is also understood by deploying concepts from diverse disciplines like Sociology, Political Science and Cultural Studies. So, there is difficulty in offering a definite account of *Dalit movement.* The present study draws from various fields to make sense of post-Ambedkarite Dalit assertion. The following study critically narrates the experience of Dalits in public institutions in post nineties by drawing from various studies. Most of the examples are drawn from the experience of Dalit assertion in Andhra Pradesh. The present study includes a broad range of examples like the university, political party, *cinema*, literature etc. An attempt is made to examine the practice of Ambedkarian ideology in the struggles of Dalits in the post independent period in the spheres of literature, *cinema*, university and political party etc. One of the features of contemporary Dalit movement is that engaged with the politics of modern public sphere, which is seen as secular space. It is the Dalit struggles and their assertion that showed the casteist brahminical character of these spheres.

With the entry of Dalits into the various public institutions, one common response is that the objectives of these public institutions have been subverted. To put it in other words, the universe of values constituting these public institutions has been thwarted. To make sense of this, one has to find a relevant conceptual framework. *Partha*

Chatterjee offers one. According to him, there are two worlds: a world of middle class constituted by modern norms of freedom of speech, voluntary associations and individual capable of choice; another is a world of subalterns constituted by other concepts which does not come under this modern bourgeoisie rubric. There is a relationship of pedagogy between the former and the latter. The entry of Dalits into modern public institutions, cause a rupture between two universes. The universe of public institutions is underpinned by modern rationality and concomitant values as created by modern-nation-state. The introduction of the universe of Dalits into public institutions results in, broadly, two consequences. It questions the nature of translation and application of modern values of *liberty* and *equality* in modern public institutions. Secondly, the visions of public institutions enter into a phase of crises of understanding and coherence. This interpretation helps us to understand the nature of hatred and conflict in public institutions. But, it also sets in other agendas of shedding the potential of *modernity* to liberate Dalits from the shackles of tradition. Dalits share an ambiguous relationship with modernity. This opens up new problems to the framework mentioned above. In this context, the present study loosely uses the above framework to narrate post-Ambedkarite *Dalit movement* in the context of various modern public institutions.

Dalits and Modernity

There are certain questions in understanding Ambedkar in relation to the process of modernity. The answer to this question has implications for the Dalit movement. Was Ambedkar supportive of modernity? If he is, what kind of modernity does he posit? Does the Dalit critique of modernity promise some kind of 'hybrid', or 'alternative' modernity? Does Ambedkar transcend the binaries of tradition vs. modernity? Does Ambedkar's thought aims at modernising tradition or does it aim at democratising tradition?

In relation to these questions, one has to understand Ambedkar in the social context he operated. As a leader of Dalits, his response to *colonialism*, Indian freedom struggle under the leadership of *Gandhi*, the Communist movement of his times and his role in the making of the *constitution* for independent India are worth considering.

Modernity is identified with Enlightenment, with the ideals of secularism, *liberalism* democracy and humanism. Modernity upholds the spirit of science and reason. It argues for a Universal Man. It considers any distinction of human beings by caste, class, region, religion, creed, gender etc. as anti modern. The western societies that have undergone through the process of industrialisation consider themselves to be modern, rational societies and others are dubbed pre modern or traditional.

Modernity is opposed to a traditional world view. Basically, tradition is vested in religion and its irrational and mythical structures. Contrary to tradition, modernity brings change in attitudes, values, orientation of thinking and the mental make up of the individual. Modernity certainly involves a break with the past. Secularism, rationalism and Universalism are the main characteristics of modernity. Reason plays a predominant role to evaluate beliefs, opinions, dogmas etc. Modernity assumes that scientific thinking should have precedence over emotions and non-rational thought. Modernity also involves changes in the socio-economic and political structures facilitating industrialisation, urbanisation and democratisation. From the economic point of view, modernity involves reorientation of the social structure bringing about material prosperity through the increasing expansion of the productive forces of society and by equitable distribution of wealth. The modern worldview is based on scientific knowledge. Modernity embraced the idea of progress and the break from history and tradition. It subscribed to a secular meaning, the demystification and desacralisation of knowledge and social organisation. It upholds the doctrines of equality, liberty and faith in human intelligence opened up by education and Universal Reason.

It is argued by some thinkers that there is a dichotomous opposition between tradition and *modernity*. *Modernity* is considered to be the anti-thesis of tradition. But many scholars, for different reasons contested the view that there is any dichotomy between tradition and *modernity*. Also, some nationalist thinkers questioned the dichotomy between tradition and *modernity*. They attempted to construct the idea of modernity differently. Nationalist thinkers argued that modernity, which is equated with industrialisation, scientific and technological advancement was limited to western countries. The so-called modernity suited colonial interests at the expense of the colonised. Keeping this view in mind, the rationale of modernity, which was put forwarded by the western colonial countries, was questioned. Indian thinkers like Gandhi and Ambedkar contested the above view from different perspectives. One can see in the thought of *Gandhi* the blend of modernity and tradition. He tried to integrate new patterns of thought and action on traditional culture. *Gandhi's* critique of western civilisation was a critique of *modernity* and his central argument is that no enduring alternative can be pursued unless that alternative negotiated to the skills, capacities and wisdom of the people.

Ambedkar too tried to overcome the tradition-modernity dichotomy. The critique of the tradition is accompanied in his refusal to accept ready made alternatives manufactured in the west. His philosophy is essentially ethical and religious and he keeps away from Western thought. And at the same time, he attacked Hinduism and its claims as religion he upholds the moral basis of life while allowing critical reason to operate. He considers *Buddhism* as the only religion which can respond to the demands of modernity and culture. Buddhist teachings he believes, appeal to reason and experience. in this sense he is critical of modernity and high lightened that priority of social reconstruction can not be achieved without taking into account the legacy of tradition. He further considers that legal and political institutions do not have a capacity to reconstruct social solidarity, and therefore tries to provide a social basis for the liberal and political ethos which does not mean an uncritical acceptance of western modernity or indigenous traditionalism.[1]

Modernity, as imposed on the third world countries has been attacked from many fronts. Modernity is considered as a necessary extension of colonialism. Modernity in India came as a package with colonialism. There is an attack on the general philosophical beliefs of modernity such as notions of Universalism and its truth claims. There is an attack on the very values of post-Enlightenment thought, on its conception of secularism and rights etc. As observed by Javeed Alam, people readily reject terms like secularism on the grounds that they are alien to and lack any affinity with 'Indian culture or traditions. However, other terms such as democracy or *equality* are readily acceptable.[2] This may give a clue to understand modernity which has taken roots in the Indian context and its complexity. This may be helpful in assessing Ambedkar.

Modern is historically embodied form of enlightenment. Whatever is entailed under enlightenment as values, beliefs, principles, ethics, morality and so on, has been thought of as universal-not just in an abstract sense but as something universalisable in the thinking and practices of all human beings. *Colonialism* has a historical connection with *capitalism* and therefore also what we have referred to as entrenched modernity. The capitalism in the colonies have demonstrative with all the features of distorted consciousness, racial superiority, arrogant cultural exclusiveness, and intellectual condescension over and above political control of those inferiors whom it has subjugated.

Monopolisation of Modernity

When *modernity* entered India, the Indian traditional intellectual community had seen it as a threat to the Indian social structure. To protect the age old brahamnical societal structure, the upholders of the tradition moved to keep the tradition intact. They started the process of monopolisation of modernity by embracing the epistemologies of modernity-such as the basic sciences and technical education. Initially, when modernity opened up new opportunities, with its inherent economic viability, the Brahmin intellectuals given up traditional epistemologies and embraced modern epistemology purely for the material prosperity. At this juncture, the whole process of embracing modernity by the intellectual community of the times, raises very interesting questions. For instance, it asks why Brahman community embraced modernity? What were the reasons for the monopolisation of modernity? Did they allow *modernity* to go into corners to transform the basic structure of the society? If it was not the case, was it the fault of 'other's, who were not able to absorb modernity? Apart from these questions there are some other interesting questions surfacing from the contemporary discourse of modernity and tradition. In contemporary debates, questions are being raised on the loss of Indian scientific models. Interestingly, the huge cry on the disappearance of Indian scientific culture was coming from quarters which had ignored these very models in the initial stages of confrontation between modernity and tradition. If it was the same community which left these very models for their fate, whom are they blaming now? Who is responsible for the loss of the Untouchables' loss of scientific and non-scientific epistemologies?

If we asses the impact of *modernity* on Indian society, the under-privileged sections of the society hardly benefited from it. If one thinks of possible reasons for this, one can easily come to the conclusion that the modernity project, in the nineteenth century, was monitored by the social elites of the times, and came from the Brahmin community. Apart from monitoring and controlling the whole process of modernisation, there were constant conscious interventions by this community to ensure their interests are secure by not allowing the fruits of modernity into other sections of the Indian society. This resulted in the halting or postponing of societal transformations. To reserve the fruits of modernity for them, they constantly realised the price of *modernity* (For instance, technical education has always remained an unreachable domain for the underprivileged sections of India). In other words, the presence of Dalits and other *sudra* communities in the scientific and educational sphere was totally absent. This is because of the complete monopolisation of modernity. Despite constant political representation from the lower caste intelligentsia of the times, the Government machinery, which was dominated by the Brahmin community in mid 1930s constantly ignored the marginalised voice. The justification given for this was the lack efficiency or lack of technical skills. However, lower caste representatives were conscious enough in asking for positions opened by the large-scale technological projects, at least for the lower position if not for the higher positions that needed technical skills.[3]

Apart from providing new avenues, *Modernity* has implications for social transformation. The elites have to overcome their own traditions and cultural beliefs. To resolve this kind of a situation they had started defending their cultural traditions and simultaneously enjoying the material benefits of the modernity at colonial times.

The relationship of the Dalits to the modern State, both colonial and post colonial, is ambiguous. It is important to re-look at political-cultural practices of Dalits to understand the Dalit response to State and modernity. If one emphasises the discursive aspects of modernity, it offers enormous possibilities to talk about Dalit suffering/ humiliation and oppression. It can also be said that Ambedkar's argument for creating a moral community is possible only if one emphasises the discursive aspects of modern experience.

The concept of *modernity* is complex. It has taken different routes in different nations and various social groups of the same nation have experienced *Modernity* differently. Many of the scholars, without any scrutiny consider that modernity came to India through British colonialism. It is contested by some scholars (like Velchuri Narayana Rao) who believe that modernisation process started quite early in India prior to colonialism. They also maintain distinctiveness of this modernity when compared to western moderntiy. For this, one has to find how modernity is rooted in India.

In the backdrop of the contemporary Dalit struggles and emergent Dalit writings, many scholars attempt to understand the relation of Dalits to modernity. How do Dalits subjectively and objectively engage with modernity?

The writings reveal that Dalit relation to *modernity* is complex. It is also, in some sense critical about the general understanding of modernity, that is modern development, science and reason. Dalit politics refuses to get incorporated into the binaries of nationalism/ *colonialism* and secularism/communalism. It also resists Universalism, the unmarked and abstract citizen as a centre of the emancipatory discourse of *modernity*. It is equally critical about the abstract 'working class'. In other words, it constantly speaks with and against both the liberal and the radical conception of man and society. Ambedkar doesn't believe in mere *individualism*, whereas the individual is the centre for liberal and modern life. He believes in community life that is rooted in a moral society and is based on the ideals of modernity. He makes differences with other *communitarians* like *conservatives* (*Hindutva* forces) and Marxists. He too believes in the religion and spiritual values and it has a marked difference with the conservatives. He argued in favour of the humanistic and the rational religion in place of 'God-centred' and dogmatic religion. His position suggests that he had a different conception of modernity in mind-that is, different from the colonial modernity of the west and the modernity imagined by the social elites of colonial and post-colonial India. Ambedkar's modernity project is invariably connected to the emancipation of Dalits. Ambedkar, as an intellectual has his own conception of modernity and at the same time as a political strategist, he engaged with the modernity mediated through western colonialism in India for the sake of the betterment of Dalits.

The trajectory of *modernity* in post-colonial India is a very complicated one. The Brahminical Hindu elite's engagement with the modernist project is quite interesting. The liberation of the self/nation is imagined in the spiritual and cultural domains. In its initial phase, Hindu nationalism started internal social reforms. The project of modernity pursued by these social elites of post-colonial India has ended up as anti-modern. As *Partha Chatterjee* notes: "...the search for the post colonial has been tied, from its very birth, with its struggle against modernity". The modernisation process carried the tag of the tradition. This ultimately led to the confrontation of secular state and the Nehruvian ideal of modernity by the Hindutva forces in contemporary times.

On the other hand, the Dalit's involvement with the colonial-mediated modernity project was too complex. In a feudal set up, where Dalits are degraded and humiliated in the name of caste and social norms, colonial modernity, to a certain extent, facilitated to become conscious of their objective condition. The institutions set by the colonialsts promised political, legal and social *equality* atleast theoretically, if not practically. In this respect, Ambedkar is in favour of the active intervention of the State to bring Dalits into the modern sphere. In early days, Brahminical social elite too felt the need for modernising Dalits. For this, they prescribed habits of 'purity' and the need for 'education' for Dalits. When more Dalits are entering the public space so far reserved for upper castes, through State-sponsored developmental programmes, it creates antagonism and conflict. With an increased assertion of Dalits and their struggles, and the marked visibility of Dalits in post-independent India has frustrated the upper castes. They pick up a new liberal language to counter the Dalits against the spirit of liberalism. For instance, when Dalits are fighting against the hegemony of caste, the upper castes dismiss this struggle as casteist. Dalits talking about caste is considered as parochial and anti-modern by them. Further, they argue for an economic basis for any emancipatory project of the state. In the anti-Mandal agitation this attitude can be witnessed. Upper castes find various strategies like this to maintain the status quo in society. Casteism of the upper castes took modern incarnation in the public sphere, and started articulating their interests in modernist discourse like, purity and pollution, 'hygiene', 'efficiency' and 'merit'.

One more interesting point is that, the upper castes started discrediting the modern political institutions in the context of the entry of Dalits into it. They go on propagating that these institutions got 'corrupted' by blaming the lower caste people. They even go on opposing the very foundations of the secular democratic state of the nation. They argue that this secular *democracy* based on the 'rationality' of western colonial model, is not based on indigenous cultural and philosophical traditions. At this point, Dalits came to the rescue of secular *democracy*. The upper caste intellectuals, by taking the post-modernist position, that 'science is a social construct', started justifying the philosophies of irrationality and dogmatism as science. It had a negative implication for Dalits. In this context, Ambedkar and Dalits of post-colonial India, are arguing in favour of the 'scientific reason' of modernity that is rooted in indigenous traditions.

In post-independent India, the *Nehruvian* project of '*modernity*', 'development', and 'progress' through big dams, heavy industries and scientific institutions benefited the upper caste groups more than anybody else. This lead to the generation of capital in India but it did not develop a capitalist culture and its values. The upper caste groups didn't come out of their feudal mindset. On the other hand, Dalits are marginalised and dislocated. This situation often meets with conflicts and tensions in the nation. Any radical assertion of Dalits is suppressed by the state. The political institutions become oppressive. Secular *democracy* may become a farce. Further, the governability for ruling class becomes a serious problem until and unless it attends the situation in a real democratic spirit.

Issues and Problems of Contemporary Dalit Movement

The movements of *untouchables* got visibility and recognition with the leadership of Ambedkar. Many untouchable communities came together and got a new identity at the national level. But there are persistent problems from the time of Ambedkar himself in building a broad based democratic *Dalit movement*. This section focuses on some of the issues and problems of the contemporary *Dalit movement*. There is no doubt that Ambedkar and his philosophy is the focal point for the contemporary Dalit movement. With the changing socio-economic conditions, Dalit lives 'too' have undergone a significant change. Dalits are asserting their rights by challenging the hegemony of the dominant castes in all spheres of life. For this, they have adopted many strategies. They have radical implications for Indian society. The potential of Ambedkar's philosophy can be understood in the wake of the Dalit movement.

From the decade of eighties onwards, a considerable number of Dalit middle class is visible in Indian society. Their presence was felt in the public sphere for the first time. They are resisting the hegemony of the upper castes in these spaces by asserting themselves in all possible ways. For the upper caste people, it was as if the space which was so far reserved for them exclusively, suddenly became uncomfortable and they are becoming irritated with the entry of Dalits into their spaces. One can see the antagonism between these two in universities, literary and cultural fields. The upper castes have suddenly picked up a liberal language to corner the Dalits. Andhra is a classic example to explain this phenomenon. The university, the city, cinema and literature are predominantly urban spaces where the above said encounters are very often witnessed.

The decade of eighties in Andhra Pradesh is known for a radical assertion of Dalits, women and the Telangana people. They have raised several questions relating to the nature of state and developmental strategy pursued by it. The *Karamchedu massacre* of 1985 and the Pro-Mandal agitations in 1991 shattered the modern secular pretensions of various social and political institutions. Around the time, Dalits became visible in public space.

Atrocities against Dalits

In Indian society, atrocities against Dalits are a very common and routine feature. It is an ongoing pan Indian phenomenon. The caste system in India is responsible for the oppression and violence against Dalits. The violence continued along with the caste system. The violence is in various forms—psychological, cultural and physical. Everyday life experiences of Dalits are horrible and humiliating. They have to face insults everywhere, whether it is a village, town, temple, school, university, function place, cinema hall, panchayat, or even parliament! It is not an exaggeration to say that there is no dignified and democratic place for Dalits to enjoy the right as a human being. They are denied access to public spaces like tanks, roads, temples and festivals. *Untouchability* is practised in different forms. First of all their houses are segregated from the main village. They are made to confine to unclean jobs. They are alienated from land and other livelihood. They are paid low wages and exploited for their labour. In the name of pollution they are not allowed access to public places. They are not allowed to sit along with caste Hindus. In hotels, they have to sit separately and separate glasses were kept for them at many places. They are not allowed into temples. Houses are not given for rent in case of Dalit employees in caste Hindus locality. They can not wear nice clothes. They must take off their chappals while walking in the localities of caste Hindus. At the time of marriage or any such occasion, Dalits are not allowed to go in procession on public roads. There is a line drawn by the caste system everywhere and Dalits are not allowed to cross it. Upper caste people routinely rape Dalit women. In the name of custom of *Jogini,* or *devadasi*, Dalit women are still sexually exploited. Dalits, for years have to work as bonded labourers at *uppercaste* landlord's house. Dalits were never called with their names in a respectable way. The uppercaste people always called them in derogatory and indecent language. In general, the violence, or atrocities against Dalits will go unnoticed. Dalits are not in a position to resist due to their low economic and social conditions. These are not the stories of yesterday. It is happening every day in India in one form or other. There are many laws to safeguard the rights of the Dalits in our Constitution. But they remain ineffective in protecting the interests of

Dalits. The state and its machinery is not in a position to come out from the dominance of the uppercaste hegemony. Even for the implementation of constitutional rights, Dalits have to struggle. They are not allowed to utilise their votes in elections. They are not allowed to contest in elections. They should not go against the will of the dominant caste Hindus of village. Even elected *they are allowed* to act as representative members and they should be subordinate to caste Hindus. Dalit houses are looted and burnt and their women are raped along with the practice of social boycott. In recent times, there are many incidents of garlanding the statue of Ambedkar (in whom Dalit's collective consciousness symbolically seen) with degrading things like footwear, by the uppercastes. As a Dalit poet P.C. Ramulu puts:

Ghayam kottakadu
Gayapadina vainame kotha
Anubhavam kotha kadu
Anubhavinchina teere kottha
(For me the Wound is not new
Only the way I got wounded is new
The experience is as past as yesterday
Only the way I got experienced is new.)[4]

(Translation mine)

With the changed socio-economic situation of Dalits, there is an assertion from the Dalit community and the atrocities against them are intensified by the upper castes. As the Dalit poet *Kalekuri Prasad* in his poem enlists the incidents of atrocities against Dalits in the contemporary times in his poem, "Pidikedu Atmagouravamkosam Talettina Vadini" (Am Raised for a Fistful of Self-respect)

Twenty years ago my name was kanchikacherla kotesu
My birth place Keelavenmani, Karamchedu, Neerukonda
Now the hardened cruelty of the landlords
Tattooed on my chest with a plough's point-Chunduru
Hence forth Chunduru is not a noun not a pronoun
Now every heart is a Chunduru, a burning

...Don't shed tears for me
If you can
Bury me in the heart of the city
Rendering the tune of life, I will bloom like a bamboo garden
Print my corpse on the page of this country
I will diffuse into the pages of history a beautiful feature
If you can
Invoke me to your hearts
Again and again I shall take birth in this very country
By becoming a struggle of wild flames.[5]

(Translation: Lakshminarasiah)

Let me explain briefly the atrocities against Dalits apart from the everyday experiences of humiliations and insults. In the mid eighties, coastal Andhra has seen a mobilisation of Dalits in the backdrop of green revolution. Some of the caste groups like kammas got benefited by green revolution and the Dalits started organising as wage labourers. The advancement of green revolution in coastal Andhra intensified the caste based polarisation and mobilisation took place from both land-owning as well as labouring communities. All the educated sections of that time were conscious of their caste.

In July 1985, *Karamchedu massacre* took place where Dalits of Madiga community were hunted down by the a few thousands of Kamma caste with axes and spears. The Dalits were attacked from all sides and the landlords brutally killed six Dalits. This incident changed the political and cultural discourse of Andhra Pradesh in a significant way. This incident followed the formation of *Dalit Mahasabha*.

In July 15, 1987 hundred of upper castes Kammas attacked Malas of Dalit community with axes, spears and sticks in Neerukonda village of Mangaligiri in Guntur district of coastal Andhra and killed four Malas and one Yadava man.

On August 6, 1991 eight Dalits of the Mala community were killed and five were injured in *Tsunduru massacre* in the coastal Andhra village of Guntur. Nearly a mob of 400 uppercaste Reddy and Telagas, armed with lathis, iron rods, knives, axes and spears descended on the Dalitwada from two directions. The mob chased the unarmed Dalits and threw six of the bodies into the drainage canals, while they packed the other two bodies into gunny bags before dumping them in the river. The issue became a national issue and has seen a large mobilisation of Dalits in protest against this incident.

These are not the only incidents of organised assaults against the Dalit community. Many incidents, similar in nature, are still continuing to happen in this country. These incidents should be read in the background of the threat posed to the upper caste hegemony by the assertion of Dalits all over the country. These atrocities can be read as a backlash against the *Dalit movement* itself.

The conscious Dalits emerged over the period of time in post-independent India asserting their identity and resisting the hegemony of the upper castes. Education of Dalits played a key role in mobilisation of Dalits, both politically and culturally.

Issue of Reservations and the Dalit Movement

It is not an exaggeration to say that the issue of reservation for Dalits in the major institutions of state is central to the *Dalit movement.* It is considered that reservations are an important means for the upliftment of the Dalit masses. In an unequal society like India, reservations are inevitable for a democratic and egalitarian society. In its constitution itself, the nation had committed for the policy of reservation, or affirmative action for certain disadvantaged social groups. But the issue of reservation is always contentious among different social groups in India. The logic may change from time to time but the essence remains the same for the social groups and its supporters and its opponents. Both in pre-independence and post-independence times, the issue is lively and the Indian politics somehow centred around this issue. In the post-independence period, the government's initiation in the implementation of the Mandal commission's recommendations for Other Backward Castes (OBCs from henceforth) in jobs and education becoming a turning point in contemporary Indian politics. Debate around the Mandal issue had direct implications for Dalits.

The development of a reservation policy in India needs a historical account. In India, certain social groups had monopoly over power, land, education, jobs and other resources at the cost of denying it to many other communities. In other terms, the wealth, knowledge, opportunities in jobs, and other resources are reserved from time immemorial to certain dominant social elites who are small in number. They maintained their monopoly by excluding the many productive communities from social, cultural, economical and political life by the strict implementation of caste system. Whatever little flexibility we have historically seen in the rigid rules and practices of caste system, it has not been because of the generosity of the social elite/ruling class.The struggles and assertion of lower castes, who are victims of the caste system made them compelled to think. Any concessions for the lower castes are a resultant outcome of such struggles from the lower castes themselves. For maintaining the unity, the ruling class was forced to take such stand to include the agitating, disadvantageous sections of society.

In the Indian context, reservations were introduced in the last decades of the nineteenth century. The subcontinent was divided into British India and many princely states. Some of the princely states were progressive and eager to modernise through the promotion of education and industry and by maintaining unity among their own people. Some of the princely states like Mysore, Baroda and Kolhapur took initiation in implementing the reservations policy and took considerable interest in the awakening and advancement of the minorities and deprived sections of society.

1. With the British and its English education, members of the affluent and newly emerging middle class people got benefited and masses remained ignorant and backward. Brahmins in the Madras presidency and the Bhadralok in the Bengal presidency took advantage of the new educational policy and the central place of the English language within it and occupied most of the posts available in the administration. Upper caste Hindus were taking advantage of the educational facilities provided by the British as well as the *Christian missionaries* and were organising and agitating for political power.

For instance, the Brahmins in Madras, comprising barely 3 per cent of the total population, occupied more than 80 percent of the posts. In the princely state of Mysore, too, the Tamil Brahmins monopolised all the jobs. Kannada Brahmins had a small share in public services. The Maharaja of Mysore advised to introduce some reforms in policy by giving larger share to the Kannadiga Brahmins, Vokkaligas and Lingayats besides the untouchable castes and the Muslims. Thus reservation had been introduced in 1918 in favour of a number of castes and communities that had very little share in administration.

The *untouchables*, or *depressed* classes had not benefited by the British education since they were kept away from education. The social custom played against them. But the British provided opportunities for untouchables as cooks, butlers, sweepers, and gardeners for the British families in their cantonments. Some of them were provided with jobs in the British army at a lower level. The *untouchables* contributed a great deal in the expansion of the British Empire. The entry of untouchables into the British army was resisted by the caste Hindus of the British army. The British were forced to reduce the untouchable's entry in Bengal army. However, the missionary's activities, such as opening of separate schools for the promotion of literacy among untouchables etc., helped these untouchable communities in many ways. This facilitated them to get access to modern institutions created by the British, though through menial jobs like peons, gangman etc.

The question of reservations in legislature for Muslims, Sikhs, Anglo-Indians, Parsis and the *Depressed classes* was discussed in the Round Table Conferences and provisions were made in the communal award of 1935. *Gandhi* opposed the specific provisions of the communal award in favour of the most deprived and disadvantaged sections of the society. He considered this identification of the *Depressed Classes* separately as a danger to Hinduism. He threatened Ambedkar that he would undertake a fast unto death on the issue of separate electorates for the *Depressed Classes*. Ambedkar, on behalf of the *Depressed Classes*, pleaded to the British to consider the *Depressed Classes* as a separate subject by ensuring measurers like, adequate representation in legislature, services and protection against discrimination, special departmental care for the upliftment of these groups etc. He presented a scheme of political safeguards for the protection of the *depressed classes* in the future constitution of a self governing India, submitted to the round table conference.[6]

Gandhi opposed any political reservations for the Dalits. He argued that Hindus had taken up the cause of the *untouchables,* and therefore, there was no reason to give them political safeguards. In fact, he had no objection for political representation of Muslims and Sikhs since they were already organised. In case of the Dalits, he argued that separate electorates worked against them since they were not organised like the Muslims and the Sikhs. If they had separate electorates their lives would be miserable in villages, which are the strongholds of Hindu orthodoxy. By giving them separate electorates you will be throwing the apple of discord between the *untouchables* and the orthodox. He had expressed in no uncertain terms that the question of separate electorates for the *untouchables* is a modern manufacture of government. The only thing needed is to put them on the voter's list, and provide for fundamental rights for them in the Constitution. Gandhi argued that separate electorates for the untouchables would ensure their bondage perpetually. Do you want the *untouchables* to remain untouchables forever? What is needed is the destruction of *untouchability* and not separate electorates. Further, he brought the example of the history of Europe to the Round Table Conference. He asked the British whether they had got separate electorates for the working classes, or women. With adult franchise, you give the untouchables complete security. Even the orthodox would have to approach them for votes.[7] Gandhi even tried to dismiss Ambedkar by saying that he was not the truly representing the untouchables. *Gandhi* claimed himself to be the real representative of the untouchables. He had understood that separate electorates that Ambedkar sought would not give him any chance for Gandhi's kind of social reform.

Ambedkar, in the capacity as the Viceroy's executive, submitted a memorandum "On the Grievances of the Scheduled Castes". With this, he demanded reservation in public services, scholarships and stipends for study within the country and abroad etc. The Viceroy duly recommended this and the Scheduled Castes were allowed 8.5 per cent reservation in central services and other facilities for the first time in the history of India in 1942. After the transfer of power in 1947, Ambedkar, as chairman of the drafting committee of the Constitution, included a provision for reservations for Scheduled Castes. Provision was made in the Constitution of India for reservation in legislature for 10 years ending in 1960. This had recently been extended up to 2010. Provision was also made for reservation in the public services. This has no time limit. This time period is always a debating point in political and civil society. 'Reservations made under article 335 read together with article 46 has no time limit prescribed under the Constitution.[8]

Initially, reservation was extended only to the members of the Scheduled Castes professing Hinduism, and some castes of Sikhism. When Ambedkar revived *Buddhism* and many of the Dalits converted to *Buddhism* they became not eligible to any of the concessions admissible to Scheduled Castes. Only in 1990, the Scheduled Castes professing *Buddhism*, were also included among the list of Scheduled Castes. Of course, there is no such restriction with regard to the people of Scheduled Tribes who return themselves as *animists*, Hindus, Christians, or Buddhists. Reservations later extended to OBCs at the national level with the implementation of the *Mandal commission* recommendations in 1993. Several states have passed their own laws in granting reservations for OBCs.

If it is *Gandhi* who worried any reservations exclusively for the untouchable will divide the Hindu society, in contemporary times, the upper caste Hindu often opposes reservations in education and government jobs for Dalits. Some of the arguments of the upper caste people against reservations are that all men are equal and why some of them should be considered differently. They bring the liberal argument that all men are equal and there should not be any differentiation in the name of caste, region, religion, or creed. But, they are using this liberal principle against its spirit. They propagate that by providing reservations to particular castes, it divides the Indian nation on caste lines. Reservations, in the lines of castes, instead of annihilating caste, will contribute further to casteism. This is one kind of argument from the upper castes as if the nation is a unified whole without having any mark of distinction in terms of caste in everyday life. They believe that the Government is encouraging caste in the name of reservation and the people who are claiming reservation wants to carry these benefits forever.

The most sophisticated argument from the upper castes is that we are not against reservations, but the criteria should be economic class. Are there not any poor people in upper castes leading life miserably? This argument would also point out the creamy layer among the Dalits. Thus they conclude that reservation is not benefiting the really poor people. It is only the affluent among Dalits who are benefiting but not the real poor. They put this argument as if they have a serious concern for the poor. They never took any agitation in favour of these very sections.

Yet another argument is that there should be a limited period for reservation. They often quote the Constitution for its time-boundness in this issue. Some arguments concern the percentage of reservation. Even the recent Supreme Court judgement reflects this mood that reservations should not exceed 50 per cent.

The most shrewd and arrogant argument from upper caste is 'merit'. Merit should be the criteria for either getting admissions, or seeking jobs. They use this 'merit' in a very limited sense in reading and writing skills in education. They never try to see merit in a broader sense by applying it to other fields of knowledge in society. Secondly, the rhetoric of anti-reservationists invokes the principle of equality against its spirit. There is an important argument to treat all human beings as moral equals in the context of civil liberties. But, states all over the world have to address socio-economic disparities of their citizens, which results in new interpretations of *equality*. Citizens with different socio-economic backgrounds might be treated differently. However, reservations facilitated the Dalits in articulating their social and political aspirations.

Dalits should be the Ruling Community

Political power is the master key to Dalit empowerment. Ambedkar visualised it as a key to the progress of Dalits. Leaders from the Dalit community tried out various possibilities to secure justice/emancipation by following different routes. In the last five decades, the experience of Dalits with parliamentary *democracy* is worth discussing.

As mentioned earlier, the community is located in the context of inhuman conditions of material existence, powerlessness in all forms of life and ideological hegemony of the dominant force of the nation. Till the day Ambedkar's wish for an emancipated Dalit community is not fulfilled, Dalits should be the ruling community of the nation. It doesn't mean that this question has lost its relevance.

There are many attempt and strategies adopted by Dalits to get the political power. Though there is a constant co-option of Dalit leaders into dominant political parties of various hues, there still exists an autonomous Dalit struggle that has even captured political power in some of the states for a short span of time. This will help us to problematise the political power vis-à-vis Dalit perception of power in the liberal democratic framework.

Political power could have two aspects, descriptive and normative. The descriptive aspect of power normally involves description regarding the different modes of exercising power in the given society. Normative aspect involves an ethical element, which raises questions of values in the exercise of power. Ambedkar's writings reveal that he puts more emphasis on the normative aspect. He, too, feels that just the independence of the nation is not any sufficient condition for political exercise. But good state should be the motive of political power. He argues that efficiency is not enough to run the government properly. What is required to hold the state is 'unselfishness' and 'impartiality' along with responsibility. As he rightly clarified regarding the political power, 'in India, the governing class has misused political power with no sense of responsibility. This power hungry insatiable class posed a serious threat to *democracy* and created imbalance in the political field.[9]

Ambedkar understood that adult franchise is not a device powerful enough to check the political power of the governing class. He fundamentally opposed the political domination of one community over the other and wanted to maintain a balance of political forces in Indian politics. He wanted to organise Dalits into a third party which he thought to hold a balance of power between rival parties.[10] Only in such situation, he felt, Dalits may have effective bargaining power.

Gopal Guru points out the similarity of Ambedkar's conception of political power with the functionalist concept of power developed by Parson. According to Parson, power is a generalised facility, or resources in society. Power is the capacity to mobilise resources in society. Parson believed that increase in the total power of society would result in the corresponding increase in the power of community, or group. Ambedkar's attempt to increase the power of Dalits through political reservations without disturbing the dominant structures in the society, by implication, amounts to the same functionalist framework, which is aimed at the institutional integration in a Parsonian sense. Ambedkar's concept of political power also implies that the distribution of power undergoes changes through which weaker sections have a chance to gain power and hence this concept has a bent of reformism.

Gopal Guru further argues that Ambedkar's theoretical framework doesn't leave any option for him to seek this politics outside the liberal democratic framework, or legal constitutional framework. He constantly emphasised that Dalits could obtain political power through compensatory discrimination embodied in the constitution.[11]

Ambedkar's political strategy revolves around two things. Firstly, he is suggesting the seizure of the political power through reservations and adult franchise within the gamut of constitutional limits, and secondly he is suggesting a broad electoral alliance of the deprived castes (alliance of OBC, ST and SC).

In the post-Ambedkar period, many of the Dalit leaders wanted political power within the framework provided by Ambedkar. Like Ambedkar, most of the Dalit leaders still considered political reservations as an effective strategy that enabled them to participate in political competition and bargaining. They considered political reservations to be a necessary device for influencing the decision making process in a liberal democracy, either at the personal level, or the Dalit community as a whole.

In fact, there is no occasion for all the Dalits elected to the legislative bodies of the country to form a united power bloc. They are divided into different parties. They have their party loyalties. Dalit vote bank, too, is divided in terms of its Dalit parties. (Maharashtra is classic example). The elected members are also not effective in their parliamentary deliberation in the issues relating to Dalits. Even in the reserved constituency, other caste groups decide their winning. It is obvious that they won't allow conscious Dalit leaders to be elected. On the other hand, any radicalisation of Dalit politics has been seen to be a threat to the dominant castes and its political parties and is immediately followed by cooption of Dalit leaders into their fold. This happened in the case of Bhaburao Gaikwad, Ramdas Athawale and other leaders of Dalit Panthers.

Ambedkar, too, hints at the liberation of Dalits outside the framework of liberal democracy and in place of it he proposed '*state socialism*'. Ambedkar wanted to establish state socialism without abrogating parliamentary *democracy* and without leaving its establishment to the will of parliamentary *democracy*. At the same time, he is against the dictatorship that undermines individual freedom. As Ambedkar said:

"The way out seems to be to retain parliamentary democracy and to prescribe state socialism by the law of Constitution so that it will be beyond the reach of parliament majority to suspend, or abrogate it. It is only by this that one can achieve and amend the triple objective; namely, to establish socialism, retain parliamentary *democracy* and avoid dictatorship."[12]

Gopal Guru argues in view of the failure of political reservations and the recent Buddhist conversion movement among Dalits that these are not adequate categories of revolutionary mobilisation. What is the immediate need of the hour is to liquidate the Hindu communal majority. For this, the Dalits in particular will have to undergo through a process in order to create a hegemonic coalition of the subaltern masses where Dalits play a key role. In other words, they have to create a political party that would go beyond the achieving of political power that would promote only the petty bourgeoisie legislators.

Bahujan Samaj Party as a New Kind of Political Party

In the late eighties, *Bahujana Samaj Party* (BSP henceforth), under the leadership of *Kanshiram*, caught the imagination of the Dalits. Within no time, in the early nineties, it got the political power in Uttar Pradesh and emerged as an important political force in North India in particular, and other parts of India in general. From the early eighties, an independent, largely anti-Congress political force, firmly based on Dalits but with a broader appeal to all backward castes and the exploited, can in fact be seen as a renewal of the earlier political trust of the Ambedkarite movement. *Kanshiram's* BSP and Prakash Ambedkar's Bharatiya Republicn Party have numerous differences in strategies and rhetoric, but they both represent the new political assertion, in which Dalits seek to emerge as leaders in a wider coalition of the exploited and marginalised. Though Kanshiram has an all India appeal to Dalits. So far, the political base of the BSP has been limited to Northern India, North-west India, to be accurate. In spite of genuine ability to appeal to other backward and minority communities, the main social base has been the large *Chamar* caste-group just as that of Ambedkar and the Republican party today whose social base is Mahars of Maharashtra. Chamars are perhaps the largest Schedule Caste in India. Leather working is their traditional occupation and like many other Dalit communities, they are largely agricultural labourers. In the west U.P., Punjab and Haryana, they confront primarily Jats as the traditional landholding and cultivating peasant caste. In east U.P. and Bihar they have to face the power of Rajputs as a non-cultivating, landlord caste and intermediary cultivating tenant castes like Kurmis, Yadavas etc.[13]

The main base for the later BSP is the BAMCEF (Backward and Minority Communities Employees Federation) which was formed in 1978. In later days, BAMCEF became the brain bank, talent bank and the financial bank of the oppressed and exploited in society. The basic objective of this organisation is to pay back to the oppressed and exploited society to which they belong. BAMCEF support later formed DS-4(Dalit Shoshit Samaj Sangarsh) in 1982. Dalit politics is spreading rapidly in northern India. In 1985, the *BSP* was formed and started contesting in elections. The *BSP* played a decisive role in U.P. and Punjab and was responsible for drawing votes away from the *Congress.* The DS-4 and BSP in the process increased their hold over Scheduled castes and Backward caste government employees. It came with the campaign:

> Vote hamara,
> Raj tumhara,
> Nahin chalega,
> Nahin chalega.
>
> (Our Vote,
> Your Rule.
> Not any more,
> Not any more.)
>
> Brahmin, Bania, Thakur–Chor,
> Baki Sab DS-4.
> (Brahmin, Bania, Thakur–thieves
> Everyone else is DS-4.)

They also came up with the slogan: "Political power is the master key."

Bhahujan Samaj Party is an institutional expression of the principle of power as a master key. For the first time, the principle of a party for Dalits, by the Dalits became a reality. It could influence through- out north India. This experiment has radically altered the nature of *democracy* and renewed the importance of election as an instrument for Dalits to express their aspirations. It radically altered the language of politics in *democracy*. It broke the patron-client relationships between the leaders and Dalit masses.

Dalit Literature

Literature is a creative rational knowledge generated by an individual/author about collective society. Indian society is a collective of heterogeneous human beings and this heterogeneity depends on a number of factors such as class, caste, gender, language, ethnicity, region, religion etc. These factors may become a source of knowledge where the individuals, or authors usually reflect upon. In the case of Dalits, the problem of caste has influenced them very much. For Dalits, access to natural resources and opportunities for wellbeing were denied naturally, or socially, because of their caste. The denial to access, restricts the Dalit individuals to a particular set of social relations for many generations and this forces them to struggle against such restrictions and change the oppressive relations. This is generally identified as a caste contradiction, or the problem of caste. The conscious Dalit individuals responded to this kind of social situation and offered a creative solution to the problems. This creative ideal model takes the form of a story, a novel, a poem or a song and is introduced back into the society. Dalit struggles around him/her influenced the Dalit writers and made them conscious of their subjective positions and in assessing the world around them objectively.

Historically, the social groups, which had acquired political and economic dominance, enjoyed the privilege over cultural production and others got silenced. Western influenced middle class, those who later played a major role in moulding the nationalist struggles, involved in the production of literary writings. It is obviously, the upper caste group's ideals and aspirations and their worldview reflected in literature too. In the post independent India, modern state was unable to uphold the promised ideals of good life and better society to the vast number of the oppressed of this country. In the political writings of literature of this time, there emerged an upper caste middle-class man as a protagonist. He is sympathetic to the lower classes and he articulates their needs and is seen to be mobilising the oppressed masses.

There are very few writings which talk about Dalits and their life. Those that exist come out as the sympathy of the upper caste writers towards labourers as a part of the class struggles. The protagonists in the literary writing is always from the upper caste groups. They are portrayed as shouldering the responsibility to reform/educate Dalits. This completely lacks knowledge about the authentic Dalit life and their experiences. These upper caste writers have constrains to perceive the lives of other communities. These socially sensitive upper caste writers could not mobilise the support of their communities to their imagined ideals and many of them moved towards spiritualism. Most of the writers came from Brahmin middle class families.

In latter days, the intensified struggles aspiring the communist ideals, too, failed to capture the Dalit imagination and the question of caste remained immune to their discourses. Till the 1980s, the entire literary discourse centred around the concept of the abstract human being, erosive of all cultural markers like caste, colour, religion, region and gender.

The radical contribution, the entry of the Dalit literary movement was to bring, is to foreground the Dalit cultural experiences characterized by humiliation, insult and suffering based on caste. By the 1980s, there emerged a considerable Dalit middle class which consists of small jobholders like teachers, clerks, constables, nurses, gangmen, hamalies and attenders. Their exposure to education and economic security opened up new possibilities in politics and literature. In the Andhra politics, *Dalit movement* is known for the innovation of a new category called Dalit, making discrimination on the basis of caste explicit. In the left parlance, the amorphous landless masses, an agricultural coolie is being replaced by category Dalit. In Gandhian terms, the word *harijan* has been pushed aside. The conceptual innovation has opened up the new ways of articulating the Dalit cause. This is clearly visible in the field of activity from theory to art.

In India, Dalit people's condition is the same cutting across the regions. There is not much difference in their social suffering and economic status. At the ground level, the forms of *untouchability* practised by the upper castes are same. They have to face humiliations, insults and discrimination in everyday life. In case of the Dalits, intervention by the state is minimal, weather it is police, or judiciary, in protecting the rights of the Dalits. They have to struggle even for constitutionally guaranteed rights. There is no option left for them other than fighting against caste hegemony. From their struggles, a literature came into existence. In late eighties, the issue of caste came to the forefront in Andhra Pradesh. This can be seen symbolically in the massacre at *Karamchedu*. As a consequence of the conscious mobilisation of Dalits, the issue related to caste got articulated in literature in late nineties. Many anthologies of poetry in the form of poetry came into the limelight. The quest for the search of their own

Dalit identity makes them broaden the literary horizons. Dalit writers questioned not only the basic premises of literature but also the epistemological positions of the existing writers. They supplied a new prism to perceive the crude reality of casteist society. With the well-debated question of representation and subjectivity, the upper caste writers were either silenced, or sidelined.

Song is the medium for Dalit literary and cultural movements from so many generations. Their folk forms centred on songs. There exists a general opinion that *Dalit literature* came into existence in late eighties. It is true that *Dalit literature,* or culture is there in the lives of Dalits. In history, there are struggles of Dalits in various forms. Dalit literature is very much enriched in oral forms and transmitted from one generation to other. It is in the form of social memory and collective memories. The written culture, or literature of Dalits may owe its existence to recent times. The pre-requisite for written culture is education. Most of the Dalits are illiterate even today. This is not their fault. They are not allowed to learn for generations. However, with limited opportunities, they have managed to enter educational institutions and have managed to get at least some small jobs. In post-independent India, a considerable Dalit middle class has emerged, though the number is small but it is significant in Indian history. This has paved the way for *Dalit literature* in the print word. Dalit writers have jolted the literary world. They raised many questions about the basic assumptions of literature on the question of authenticity and representation. Their entry, dismantled all the literary canons. They declared that we will write about ourselves. Telugu literary society has witnessed the silence of the existing upper caste writer, weather it is Brahminical, or progressive writer. Any new struggle, or literature brings new symbols and new language. It is same with the Dalit movement and *Dalit literature*. It is in Andhra that Dalit writers are confronted with the ideologies of alternative struggles in the issue of caste. Here serious debates, confrontations and negotiations in *civil society* are taking place among different literary and political camps.

Mostly, the questions centred on who are Dalits? What is Dalit literature? What is the ideology of the *Dalit movement* and Dalit literature? One Dalit anthology of poetry named *Chikkanavutunna*

Pata (1995)[14] came with a proposition that SC, ST, BC and Minorities are also called Dalits. At the same time, another anthology named *Dalit Manifesto* (1995)[15] proposed that, the labourers who are suppressed culturally, politically and economically are called Dalits. They didn't include Muslim writers in their anthology by justifying that though Muslims are victims of Hindu religion as Dalits, they cannot be considered under the category of Dalits. Secondly, whatever is written by the Dalits are considered as Dalit literature. *Dalit Manifesto* argued that, whatever was written with Dalit consciousness could only be considered as *Dalit literature*, but not the other way. The *Dalit Manifesto* become controversial by considering the latter and for inclusion of progressive upper caste writers who are conscious of Dalit problems. In course of time, this controversy resolved itself by considering whatever is written by the Dalits with their social experience is only qualified to be *Dalit literature*. The non-Dalits writings about Dalits may be treated as sympathetic for the cause of Dalits, but not considered as *Dalit literature*. For the liberation of Dalits, Dalits will have to achieve political power only through the struggle but not by appealing to the state. Some others consider that it is not necessarily through the means adopted by radical left parties but also through various other means like capturing power through parliamentary means. On the question of ideology, there are different opinions. *Desiya Marxism* is one such dominant opinion, the Marxist philosophy that is internalised thinking of Ambedkar and *Phule*.

Later came the *Padunekkina Pata* (1996)[16] an anthology of poetry. It declared that Ambedkarism is the only ideology for the liberation of Dalits. In all these controversies, one can see the confrontation, or negotiation with the then existing alternative political struggles. One of the responses was that Dalit literature was saying that it is a part of revolutionary literature.[17] Some of the scholars of the Marxist camp considered the problem of caste as a class problem. There is another argument that both are different literary movements. "Dalit writers consider the caste as an economical, social and political system. Whereas revolutionary writers consider caste as a social problem."[18] Dalit literary movement is autonomous and in no way related to *Marxism*. "The aim of revolutionary literature is economic *equality* and it is a casteless society for *Dalit literature*. For the emergence of *Dalit literature*, revolutionary literature may have facilitated; but it is improper to say that both are the same."[19] There emerged another opinion that though both of them are not related, there is a need to struggle in a united way against oppression.[20]

The literary expression of Dalit writers started with poetry, which has enjoyed power over other forms. To suit the authentic expression of their lives they also selected the other forms like 'short story' and 'novel'. The inner urge, or struggle within them has propelled them to write short stories and novels. This is a significant transformation of Dalit writers. At least, it creates confusion in locating history. Novel and short story not only broadened the canvas of the writers and made them accountable to history. The Dalit writers probed the history and brought into the literary world many things, which were not touched earlier the other by upper caste writers. In fact, Dalit writers narrated the submerged culture, philosophy and histories of the Dalits. The political discourses of Marxian revolutionary and feminist movements also influenced the Dalit novelists. It made them sensitive to other struggles, while writing about Dalits. Wherever it is necessary, they differed with Marxian revolutionary politics and its practices. The rise of sub-caste consciousness among the Dalits helped the writers to speak about the concrete lifestyles of Dalit's sub-castes rather than political rhetoric and language of the given time. Dalit novel may be said to be the culminating point of all the political movements since Dalit novelist has internalised the essence of all these struggles.

However, in the decade of the nineties, a good number of Dalit writers have come to the forefront. Most of them are of the age group of 25-35 years. They have touched all the spheres of life from a caste point of view. For example, early writings in Telugu consider the life of rickshaw pullers and prostitutes and treated them sympathetically for their low economic status. *Dalit literature* depicted the same from a Dalit point of view. Through literature, Dalit writers gave attention to concrete life experiences of Dalit lives that had so far not been touched by anyone in Telugu literature. Some of the newspapers have encouraged *Dalit literature*. Where the *Dalit movement* is at a low profile, there the Dalit writers kept the Dalit issue alive. *Dalit literature* introduced fresh tones to Telugu literature. The idiom and expression is new to Telugu literature. They brought the respect to native Dalit dialect. The Dalit writers shattered the constructed myths in literature both in form and content. Literature came close to their life. It occupied the political space and even tried to articulate all the problems.

The *Madiga Dandora* movement for the categorisation of SC reservation proportionate to the population of sub-caste triggered a new kind of articulation in the *Dalit movement* as well as in Dalit literature. The logic of representing one's own self led to fragmentation in Dalit literature. It is understood that writing about one's caste experience is the only authentic representation. Dalit writers were forced to write and represent their own caste. In one way, this atmosphere enriched Dalit literature by representing themselves. On the other, it weakened the force of Dalit writings. Most of the Dalit writers of *Mala* community become silent within no time. Some time, the *madiga* writers were on the centre-stage when they wrote about their life struggles. *Chandala Chatimpu, Madigodu* (The Stories of Madiga's life) of Nagappagari Sundar Raju and *Mallemoggala Godugu* (The Umbrella of Jasmines) of Yendluri Sudhakar are worth mentioning. Writers, who belong to backward castes, too, got separated from the earlier Dalit identity and became confined to their own community life. They brought an anthology of poems with a name of *Ventade Kalalu (Haunting Pens)*. Muslim writers also made a conscious attempt to assert their own identity. They came with a poetry collection named *Jaljala*. Dalit women, too, started questioning the oppression of caste and patriarchy of Dalit males and this got articulated in literature. *Nallapoddu* (The Black Dawn) is an exclusive collection of Dalit women's writings.

At end of the decade of nineties, Dalit writers who are active in writing poetry are slowly disappearing from Telugu literary scene. There are other reasons for the silence of *Dalit literature*. One is that, there is no significant Dalit movement and political leadership. The Dalit writers, who mostly came from the middle class, are limited to their urban life and somewhere lost their roots. There is competition among Dalit writers and their career orientation is also responsible in diluting Dalit literarure. There is no political, or public check on Dalit writers since there is no political struggle. Thirdly, Dalit writers, are mostly confined to poetry and they didn't take effort in other forms like story, novel, song and autobiography forms. They succeeded in tapping their rich literature from oral traditions. Finally, the upper caste media was not showing interest like earlier days in encouraging *Dalit literature*.

At this historical juncture, some of Dalit writers shifted to the other genres like story, song and novel to construct their cultural past and struggles of the community. They, too, realised that nothing is available about them in government documents and literary, cultural works. To win the political struggles Dalits need to be armed culturally. *Kalyana Rao's* novel *Antarani Vasantham* (2000)[21] is a landmark in Dalit literary and cultural history from the Dalit point of view. The novel recorded the collective social experiences and struggles of Dalit community. The social memory of a community, transmitted over generations, has been put in a written form. The novel is a written social document of Dalit culture, which is predominantly in oral tradition. This novel is an attempt to search a collective identity of the Dalit community. It is the chronicle of life of six generations of Dalits. This records a hundred years' struggle of the Dalit communities. In the context where the elite scholars do not consider lower caste people's struggles, culture, philosophy, life styles and history, this novel becomes the source book for culture, history, politics and philosophy of Dalits. *Kalyana Rao* explained how the Dalit culture is born from the lower caste people's involvement in labour. They spontaneously and naturally composed the songs from their life. Apart from the value of entertainment, the Dalits used cultural performance symbolically as a social protest against the dominance of hegemony of upper caste social groups. It explains Dalit struggles in various forms in a given social conditions. The novel depicts not only the sufferings of Dalits but also joyful moments in their life. This novel is an attempt towards writing history, philosophy, politics and culture of Dalits in a a comprehensive form. In *Antarani Vasantham*, constraints to freedom of Dalits, come from an enemy who is an upper caste. The idea of freedom itself indicates for Kalyana Rao, a perpetual flow of resistance by Dalit community to an upper caste community. Dalit community has been described as a focal point of creativity, resistance to oppression and a character of purity.

Yendluri Sudhakar's Malle Moggala Godugu is a collection of autobiographical stories from the Dalit community. It is the Dalit poet Sudhakar's search for his community roots where a rich cultural tradition and indigenous knowledge systems were enlivened. To write these stories he went to his native village and recorded the social and cultural experiences of older generations. *Vemula Yellaih's* novel *Kakka* is a Dalit boy's struggle for *madigisation*. He learns to play *Dappu* from the community's head as a symbol of pride of the community. This novel, not only discuses the Dalit struggle against the upper caste hegemony, but also finds the problems within Dalit community. In the Telugu literary world, the Dalit novel is the culmination point of all the alternative struggles. It internalised the struggles of Dalit sub-castes, women and naxalite movements.

The Dalit writers may have failed to take the literary, cultural movement further. But, the questions raised through literature are fresh and haunts the political movements of our contemporary times in all possible ways. All the upper caste writers ranging from Brahminical to progressive writers has compelled to take note of it.

Cinema and Dalits

Cinema is the culmination point of entertainment (art) and technology. It came to India as a product of *modernity*. It emerged as a powerful and popular media by pushing aside all other cultural forms. Cinema, too, has undergone many changes both in production and reception with changing social and political contexts. Every cinema has its social, political and historical context. It is the same as with its audience. *Cinema*, from its inception, is in the hands of the capitalist classes. It responds, or mediates in its own fashion to the problems and struggles of the society. *Cinema*, as the cultural form of dominant classes/castes has to negotiate and re-frame the dissent according to the dominant ideology. It is necessary to look into the strife ridden social situation through cultural forms, through cinema especially.

One can take note of the diverse ways of representing Dalits in *cinema* and the receptions of those images by Dalits as audiences. The circulation and reception of cinema is situated in particular historical, social and political contexts. The meaning of popular culture exists only in their circulation, not in the texts. As *Ien Ang* puts, audience are seen as producers of meaning not just consumers of media contexts. They decode or interpret media texts in ways that are related to their social and cultural circumstances and to the way in which they subjectively experience these circumstances' In the given social and cultural context, the Dalits' look at cinema makes sense to understand their political impulse.

The form of the nation is produced in the struggle by/with its various institutional manifestations. Scholars working on Indian political process have increasingly drawn the conceptual tools from the Gramscian notion of passive revolution. According to Gramsci, social transformation occurs through gradual, incremental changes in the social formation, unlike the bourgeoisie's revolutions of France and England. In this instance, bourgeoisie is weak, unable to transform the social formation from the feudal shackles on its own. Hence, the bourgeoisie enters into an alliance with the feudal classes and rich peasants and bureaucrats. This alliance is negotiated and renegotiated over a period of time. These conflicts between the ruling bloc, along with the subaltern struggles, in their various internal equations used to manifest in cinema.

In Andhra Pradesh, the hegemonic bloc in the fifties constitutes the nascent bourgeoisie, feudal landlords and the emerging rich peasant. The State initiated land reforms met with little success. The general wish of *Nehruvian* reforms of feudal structure was seen in early cinemas of fifties. Later green revolution produced huge agrarian surpluses and wage labour. This agrarian surplus owned by the upper caste (especially Kamma community) has turned into capital for cinema. Around the same time feudalism received serious blows from the Naxalite movement. The corresponding cultural form is a depiction of crisis in feudalism through *N.T. Ramarao's* films, followed by a void of feudal patriarch. This was filled by Telugu nationalism. Later in the eighties, the rich peasant who also invested in cinema, tries to depict the situation of a hero as an agent of condemning feudalism and assigning legitimacy to State. This can be seen as the popular expression of anti feudal struggles. Green revolution also had the seeds of assertions of Dalits, which happened through wage labour and state development programmes. This culminated in the *massacre* of *Karamchedu*, where five Dalits were killed by upper castes (Kamma). An equally significant event, disturbing the foundation of modern secular State, is the Mandal agitation. These incidents are the symbols of increasing expression of Dalits in public spaces from which they were hitherto excluded. In representing the turmoil it has been increasingly difficult for dominant ideology to produce itself. The hero of the cinema mostly representing the subaltern is travelling through various routes, and in the climax used to resolve the crisis.

Travelling through the disturbed zones of social turmoil, the lower caste hero confronts the upper caste female, which has generated a lot of anxiety among the middle class upper caste audiences. It has become increasingly difficult for the film industry to produce a film acceptable to all the audiences, which is posed a crisis of the mass film. This has been met with several responses. One is increasing the importance of storyline, second one is reshaping of star image.

By late eighties, *cinema* had undergone significant changes with changes in society. On the one hand, there are struggles of working class, lower caste groups, Adivasis and women for their rights. On the other hand, liberalisation policies and the ideology of Hindutva was influencing the Indian society.deeply Most importantly, social groups of India became polarised after Mandal politics and it is the same with the audience of the cinema. For the film industry, it became a difficult task to satisfy or accommodate all the audiences. Especially the mass cinema of Telugu and Tamil languages were in crisis. The middle class complained endlessly about the mass hero and the excessive obscenity in films. The middle class preferred to keep away from cinema halls and accused that they could no more watch the cinema with family. In this kind of an atmosphere, there were efforts from new directors to change the image of the hero with a somewhat 'realistic' story line up. They were successful in bringing the middle class again into the cinema halls. Directors like Mani Ratnam, Ramgopal Verma and Shankar were the pioneers of this 'new middle class political cinema'. The secret behind the success of these directors is that they exactly reflect the aspirations and anxieties of the newly emerged middle class of the late eighties. The films appear like a response to everyday struggles that are happening around us and are packed with sophisticated techniques. Every frame of the film is loaded with consumer culture. All films pose as if they are discussing serious political issues of the contemporary times.

This new middle class belongs to the second generation of independent India. Their dreams always revolve around 'America' and their soul revolves around 'Bharat'. They are the staunch votaries of consumer culture and are close to the urban life styles. The philosophy they believe is the mantra of 'hard work' and 'merit'. They try to appropriate the legacy of the progressive values of the social reformers. In practice, though they act against the spirit of heroes/symbols of social reformers, they consider them as their property of natural inheritance. They could not tolerate any visibility of the lower caste groups in any public space. They treat them as 'inefficient', 'incompetent', 'manner-less', 'violent', 'corrupt', and ultimately a hurdle to the development of nation. Whenever the lower caste people bring the discussion of 'caste' and its oppression, this urban upper caste, middle class treats them as 'casteist' and 'narrow' by elevating themselves as 'modern'. For the sake of the nation, they consider it is their duty to eliminate 'these corrupt and casteist politics'. They always give the impression that they are for the protection of the nation and ready to sacrifice for the nation. Who fulfils this kind of ideology is the real hero for them, both in real life and cinema.

In the post nineties, as a response to economic liberalisation and Hindu fundamentalism, the revival of local culture/traditions has been shown as a resolution of the problem. This can be seen in the films of S.V. Krishna Reddy and *Krishna Vamsee* in different forms. At the same time, Andhra Pradesh emerged as an agent of 'change', 'progress' and 'modernisation'. There also emerged a consumerist middle class audience totally devoid of any social concern, as propagators of the ideology of the State in the liberalisation era. The films of Mani *Ratnam, Shankar* and *Rama Gopal Verma* reflect this. At the same time, parallel to this trend, the semi radical films with the themes of tribal struggles too got success (*Yerra Sainyam, Ose Ramulamma*). It showed that the institution of cinema becomes a place for the contestation of the claims of various social groups. There are occasions of public confrontations on the depiction of lower caste groups in negative roles. Cinema halls were burnt on the release of film Shool of the *Ramagopal Verma* school in which a lower caste political leader was represented in a negative role. Apart from these kinds of confrontations, cinema hall itself is a place of reflection of the hierarchy of the social system. There are invisible bundaries existing in the seating in cinema halls. The demarcation seems to be in the lines of the purchasing power of tickets but the tension prevails when one cross the limits. In an incident in a cinema hall, an educated Dalit boy touched by mistake an upper caste man sitting next to him *in the balcony class*. This lead to the *Tsuduru massacre* and thus shows the social meanings of seating arrangement in cinema halls.

The new constellation of social forces can be grasped through the way an institution like the *cinema* manages social contradictions in the process of narrating the story. It also provides interesting insights if one looks at the nature of reception of films close to the familiar markers of social divide.

The University and Dalit Struggles

The university is a modern public space. Till the eighties, the entry of Dalits into the University was minimal. From the eighties onwards, there is a visibility of Dalit students in the University. The entry of students from lower caste groups is possible only because of the reservations in educational institutions. Mostly, they are confined to the Social Sciences and the Humanities. There is a serious debate begun in academic circles about the lowering of academic standards in higher education. For the Dalits, it is a new experience in the University. They are usually confronted with the existing academic and cultural environment of the University, which is new for them. On the other side, upper caste students feel threatened with the very entry of Dalit students. There is a strong feeling prevailing among these students that Dalit students are grabbing their opportunities in the name of reservations without having any 'merit', or taking any effort towards it.

As a result, one can see a serious confrontation between the students from lower caste groups and upper caste groups in the context of competition for resources and opportunities. This can be seen in the agitations around the implementation of *Mandal commission* recommendation for ensuring the reservations for OBCs in government jobs. This created almost a polarisation of Indian society in the lines of caste. Mandal issue was a turning point in Indian politics. The inherent contradictions on the issue of caste came into public debates. This episode influenced the *civil society* in general and university campuses in particular. A serious politicisation began in the universities and students became conscious of their castes, rather pretend to be ignorant of caste.

To understand the Mandal and Post-Mandal politics in a public space like the university, the developments in the university of Hyderabad and the political assertion of Dalit students in the university for a decade may provide some insights. This university produced many Dalit writers and scholars in contemporary times. This University is known for its immediate response to the political happenings of India, rather any other university in Nineties. Dalit politics outside the campus particularly influenced the university.

University of Hyderabad as a central university came into existence in the late seventies in Hyderabad, Andhra Pradesh. It was established as per the six-point formula intended to concede to the demands of Jai Andhra movement. It was assumed that the university may provide opportunities for higher education to people from all regions of A.P. since another university in Hyderabad, Osmania University, predominantly catered to the needs of the Telangana region. At present, the University has been able to attract students from all over India, though the majority of them are from A.P. The location of the university assumes importance, as A.P. has been known for intense political struggles like the Naxalite movement and contemporary Dalit and women struggles. Students of the neighbouring Osmania University had gone to villages to participate in rural-peasant struggles in Telengana in the eighties. That was the atmosphere surrounding the University at the time of its inception. But the University of Hyderabad has been immune to all those political influences throughout the eighties.

While conceiving the idea of that university, the underlying premise was primarily to promote excellence in the field of Sciences, and it was followed by Social Sciences and then the Humanities. Semester system was introduced and retained till now to monitor the performance of the students closely. Teachers have been given total autonomy in the matters relating to curriculum, teaching and evaluation. The medium of entrance examination is only English. These things heavily influence the social composition of the university and the retention of students from relatively disadvantageous social background. But precisely this has become essential to the identity the University advertises to enhance its reputation. Throughout its career, the university had a significant number of students from the elite and upper middle class back ground. This university fulfilled the upper caste, middle class dream of studying in an island of excellence where pursuit of knowledge is to promote one's career alone. Majority of university teachers come from elite social backgrounds who have studied in 'prestigious' institutions. But they do carry notions of unbridled academic pursuit as short cut to serve the developmental needs of the society. Everything else appears to disturb this middle class aesthetic of calm, pleasant campus devoid of 'dirty' politics. Everything seemed to be 'fine' in those early days.

Till late eighties, students used to organise around their classroom. His/her department or batch, marked the student. One is identified by the names of few individuals visible in public. Disadvantages associated with particular social background like one's caste, economic position, rural/urban and cultural (un) skills associated with them were never openly talked about. They were pushed under carpet and made beautiful by the cosmetic liberal environment. Dissent was limited to private murmurs. Collective activity was centred around picnics, fresher's and farewell parties. The idea of discomfort over elite ways of life were partly expressed in terms of particular depts or groups; For instance, English dept. students had the image of being hip/arrogant. In those days, the enrolment of Dalit students into P.G. courses was minimal. Most of the Dalit students used to drop out of their courses as soon as their first semester got over, as they were not given with the required percentage of marks. Of course, the drop out rate used to vary from department to department. Students from the Dalit community didn't have any other option, except to exit from the university. It was rare to find Dalit students with 50 per cent of marks in those days. It was accepted as one's fate, which cannot be changed by conscious human effort. The enrolment of Dalit students into research was almost negligible since the rule of reservation was not followed in case of admission into research programmes.

Things started changing by the end of eighties. There had emerged a class of students from the Dalit communities whose parents had been employed in small government jobs. This can be mentioned as the product of efforts of *Christian missionaries* and welfare policies of the postcolonial government. These students were able to study in some of the good colleges located in the developed coastal region of the State. They had entered into the campus by the late eighties. This phenomenon has become regular and irreversible.

Break through in the political situation of the campus came up with the announcement of *Mandal commission* recommendations providing 27 per cent of reservations in employment for OBCs. This has resulted in nationwide hysteria among the upper castes who went protesting against the government move. Upper caste students within the campus also joined/led the mobilisation with the active participation of women. University of Hyderabad's upper caste students spearheaded the anti-Mandal commission forum (A.M.C.F.) at the state level in Andhra Pradesh. They came up with the articulation that these (OBC/Dalit) students would breed inefficiency in governmental institutions. For instance, bridges built by them are bound to collapse and if they become doctors, they will surely end up killing the patients as they are necessarily inefficient. As a consequence the country will go to dogs. *Aren't there many poor people within upper castes? Why not economic criteria? Aren't we all human beings?* These were basically the arguments against reservations on the basis caste. They do describe OBC/Dalit students as inefficient and at the same time they staunchly refute the idea of reservation on the basis of caste. *How can you blame us for something, which our forefathers have done? Any way we are not practising untouchability*. That was the attitude of upper castes on campus as well as all over the country.

Anti-Mandal commission forum (AMCF) from the university has become prominent in many of the activities conducted against Mandal commission report in Hyderabad. This has precipitated a strong feeling of hurt, indignity and insult prominently among the Dalit students and a few OBC students. There was a sense of hurt as Dalit students were referred in derogatory terms in AMCF articulations. As a response to AMCF, a few students had pasted poems by progressive writers in defence of reservations. (Janachaitany Vedika's poems and Varavara Rao's *Dejavu*) on the walls. Then, the students from Dalit communities at the centre and a few OBC and sympathetic progressive students among the upper caste together formed an organisation, *Progressive* Students Forum (PSF). Prior to this, there was an informal discussion on naming the organisation, whether SC,ST and BC Students Welfare Association or some other name. The Dalit students began programmes of protest against AMCF. Dalit students took it as a point to attend the classes when AMCF called for boycott of classes. AMCF students had regular programmes in the city of Hyderabad like *dharnas, shoe polishing, sweeping roads* etc. to prove that they would be "reduced" to doing menial jobs if Mandal commission recommendations were implemented. The university authorities supposed to be neutral, provided them with buses to go to the city comfortably. That was pointed out and made public by the PSF. There was an encounter between a huge procession of democratic organisations of the state and few AMCF students who hijacked a bus to go for a dharna. The AMCF students shouted slogans against the people in procession. People in procession had come to the bus and gave few blows to AMCF students in bus. The AMCF in the university alleged that goons hired by the PSF had resorted to violence. At that time, the union minister P. Upendra visited the campus on an official function. Students of AMCF tried to disrupt the meeting and entered into a fierce verbal confrontation with him. PSF students intervened and defended the government's decision. After a few days, the PSF called for a university bandh. Dalit students sat at the main gates of the University to block the entry into and exit from the university. Then AMCF students came and just walked over Dalit students. Dalit students confronted them forcefully. University declared vacation immediately in order to diffuse the crisis.

That can be mentioned as the first instance of direct confrontation between the Dalit students and others (AMCF) in an otherwise peaceful campus. It had become clear and open to the campus, who is who. The silence was broken by the upper caste students and timely responded by the Dalit students. There had emerged a kind of polarisation between the Dalits and others. Despite of this polarisation, there have been few upper caste individuals, who were with the PSF and actively participated in it. This polarisation had made explicit the deeply ingrained attitudes of upper castes towards Dalits. It has caused semantic rapture and radically changed meanings associated with Dalits. There was a tendency to indicate SC/STs with PSF in informal conversation. Immediately after the vacation, whatever happened during Mandal agitation period was thrown into the realm of the private of the upper castes, it was never again discussed in public so enthusiastically. But the spectre of PSF continued to haunt them. PSF formed in the context continued to take up various academic and socio-political issues. It has given a sense of confidence to Dalits to be comfortable in campus and to express one's problems and demand for resolving them. This atmosphere helped to raise several questions relating to inbuilt biases within the academic system.

With the active emergence of the PSF, Students' Union of the University lost its importance. Students' Union is an elected body and supposed to represent all the students. The students, union is was the sole authority on matters relating to students. The emergence of separate category PSF made students union irrelevant as PSF thought that they will represent themselves separately. The space of discussion and debate is also taken up by PSF by its innumerable public meetings. So the Students, Union became hallow and left to perform only functions like organising orchestras on occasion of freshers parties, arranging buses to city on the occasion of UGC NET and civil services examinations etc.

On the other hand, PSF began to question the casteist biases built into notions of academic standards and merit. They took up instances of students who were not passed or those who had got less mark. They have highlighted how Dalit students had been excluded from classroom interaction and active student-teacher relationship because of the implicit ease and comfort in their relationship among upper caste teachers and students. This was made possible for the upper castes with their English accent, body language and cultural skills. This has resulted in a severe exclusion and isolation from classroom. As a result, Dalits were considered as students unfit to be students in this 'prestigious' university. This process of exclusion and finally awarding grades was made an issue by PSF. This was articulated as one of the important discriminations in academic institutions on the basis of caste. PSF submitted memorandums to authorities, issued pamphlets on these cases and talked to various departments.

PSF was born and had grown in quite a turbulent time in Indian politics. It was bound to negotiate and cope with the various challenges that have come to the forefront during and after *Mandal commission* agitation. One is the growing communalisation of Indian society centred on Babri Masjid demolition. The second one is liberalisation and privatisation of the economy and its associated evil impact on the education sector. Thirdly, proliferation of politics based on identities (caste, gender, region, religion, language etc.). The campus witnessed endless debates and discussions over communalisation and privatisation issues during that period with education in the central focus. PSF tried to build opinion against the Dunkel proposals through pamphleteering and public discussion. At the time of the *Tsundur massacre* of Dalits (1991), PSF collected relief to the tune of 80,000 rupees and went over there to stand with the victims of massacre. In the PSF initiated discussions, the then public intellectuals associated with civil liberties and radical left used to participate. The practice of pasting pamphlets on walls has become regular from then onwards. There was never an idea of leaders representing the organisation while speaking to authorities. Almost all the members of the organisation used to go at once at the time of speaking to authorities. Thus, there was no secrecy and no idea of particular leader heading the organisation. PSF has contested elections to the students' union once on its banner. That was the only instance of students contesting elections on behalf of the organisation. One of its contestants won as general secretary. During the elections, upper caste groups conducted negative campaign against PSF. The nature of campaign was vilifying. PSF. PSF was blamed for politicising the campus. They were marked as hate categories by branding them as 'SCs', 'Naxalites', 'trouble makers', 'violent people' etc. Strong animosity was built against the PSF. In that situation, one of the members of the PSF spontaneously reacted and thrashed two people who were active in the hate campaign against the PSF. Then the entire campus reacted by moving in hundreds, shouting slogans like down with the gooodaism of PSF. These kinds of mobilisations were quite new to the campus. These kind of isolated instances by Dalits were blown beyond proportions and students asked for rustication or some form of stern punishment. Upper castes demanded for the banning of the organisation as well. This is how the upper castes repeatedly responded to isolated instances. Authorities have taken this support as an opportunity to demolish the organisation and to silence its political voice. Following this, two important members of the PSF were denied seats in the Ph.D. programme. While protesting this, the authorities deployed the police outside the V.C.s chamber and created terror among the students.

By this time, there had already emerged a separate voice of women. A group of women came together to form an organisation, Women Students Forum (WSF). This forum mainly comprised students from the English department belonging to other states than AP. They were more vocal, convent educated, urban-based, middle class, independent and confident. They have basically taken up issues of sexual harassment and made explicit the silence surrounding issues relating to women in a situation of apparently joyful life. They have faced lot of negative campaigning with unsigned posters and by actively circulating rumours about them. Once some of the members of WSF were sent pornographic mails, apparently to threaten them and dissuade them from activism. These kinds of techniques with fresh innovations are still followed to dissuade women from activism. Campus had been hostile to issues of women. They haven't got any kind of support from authorities while facing hostile campaigns. They have brought in patriarchy into the campus political discourse as a critical conceptual tool. There had been a tendency to tie PSF and WSF together by the general public as both were dissenting groups in campus. In some of the issues WSF and PSF worked together.

The decade of nineties is known for the autonomous Dalit movement in Andhra Pradesh. It was also the time around which craving for a strong identity had emerged in Dalit politics. In campus, in PSF the markers of distinction were loose. There has always been scope for non-Dalits participating in it. The ideological, political expression was informed by debates. As against this, Dalits came together and started a separate organisation for themselves in the year 1994, with membership exclusively being given to students belonging to SCs and STs. It was named after B. R. Ambedkar, i.e., Dr. B.R. Ambedkar Students Association (hereafter ASA). It involved a separate expression of Dalit political and cultural identity. Students of SC and ST communities have strongly involved and participated in this organisation and evolved a new collective life. The PSF was weakened with the shift of support of Dalits to ASA.

Around this time, a separate cultural and literary organisation named Visphotana had come into existence. It enabled and encouraged students to write poetry and engage in discussions over current trends in Telugu literature like Dalit, feminist and revolutionary literature. It has conducted seminars, poetry-meets and ran wall magazines containing poems of outstanding Telugu writers as well as poems by students. A considerable number of women students also participated in its activities. This organisation became the literary articulation of the agony of many Dalit students and produced a good number of writers in Telugu literature in later times. This literary organisation filled the vacuum left by the PSF in negotiating the different political identities of campus.

In the mean time, two shocking incidents happened on campus in the year 1995, one was the suicide of a Dalit women student and the other, a rape of an upper caste woman student on campus. These two incidents generated a lot of political debate among the various groups of students. Students mobilised in their struggle against these incidents with their respective political stand.

A Dalit women named Suneetha had committed suicide after being betrayed by an upper caste student who had promised to marry her. People across political spectrums participated in the beginning. Later PSF, ASA and WSF together led the agitation and had gone to the village of the upper caste student and campaigned in the village to boycott the family of the accused. In support of this, they mobilised the local democratic organisations. An enormous amount of debate took place among the organisations involved in the issues. They have analysed the issue varyingly as per one's perspective as involving caste or gender as the primary analytical category. ASA considered this issue as primarily a caste issue and later a gender issue. Women Students' forum considered this issue as primarily gender and then caste. PSF considered this as caste, gender and class issue. Where as other upper castes considered this as a humanistic issue rather than any other. Visphotana has brought out a booklet containing the poems written on this issue by the students on campus, named as *Suneetha Poddunne Posterai Palakristundi*.

Another incident that lead to a lot of political debate happened on August 15, 1995. That day, some villagers from one of the villages that surround the university, raped a woman student on campus. The campus as a whole was shocked. All students agitated for the nabbing of the culprits immediately. There were regular meetings on the campus to discuss the future course of agitation on this issue. The important idea that had come up for discussion was that women should be given leadership as it involves intricate matters relating to women's dignity and since it is a 'women issue'. There was another view, predominantly from the men -that there should be equal representation of men and women and described it as 'human issue'. All the campus organisations were actively participating in this struggle. ASA had put as one of its demands an exgratia of two lakh rupees to the rape victim in its pamphlet supporting the agitation. The demand of exgratia created havoc among the upper caste, middle class women of the campus. They got irritated. They demanded an apology for mentioning a 'price for women's *dignity*'. In that charged atmosphere one of the faculty commented, 'we are so insensitive to women, let us accept that all men are bastards, including me'. This caused an enormous frustration among men and a big procession took place to attack that faculty member. They demanded that the faculty member should be suspended immediately. The women students as whole came in support of that particular faculty and from men only few individuals of PSF came in protecting the faculty from a mob attack. That led to huge processions and counter processions over this issue. Men and women were totally divided on this issue. There was no talk between men and women even among friends for a few days. The main issue got sidetracked. The point to note here is that the Dalit students of ASA were compelled to turn against women and upper caste men came in support of ASA in the name of 'men's pride'. This reveals inbuilt contradictions and possible political alliances in the given context. In the following elections to the students' union a Dalit student got elected with a huge margin (not a member of ASA) against a woman who contested from the PSF banner who lost. The guess is that women didn't vote to a women candidate even after such a sharp divide.

Let me explain the issues involved and the functioning of ASA. ASA has gradually become the sole representative voice of the Dalit community on campus. The ways of expressing solidarity among Dalit community has assumed new ways. A huge gathering takes place on the occasion of the birth and death anniversaries of Ambedkar every year. This is the spectacle through which the strength of the Dalits is shown in public. A strong network of Dalit students was established in each and every hostel through forming hostel committees and celebrating Ambedkar anniversaries through them. They continue the fight against attitudes of awarding less marks by upper caste teachers, which PSF had done earlier. They have put sustained pressure on the authorities to follow reservations. They demanded seats for Dalit students in research every year as it has become a common practice in selections to leave the seats of SCs and STs vacant.

To strengthen itself, ASA usually projects the PSF, as a Naxalite leaning students organisation. It consciously tried to keep Dalit students out of the fold of PSF. Involvement in PSF was seen to be inviting the unnecessary risk of police involvement. This was to confront with the informed political debates from outside ASA. The speakers invited for the functions were Dalit ministers, successful Dalit officers and Dalit leaders like Katti Padma Rao. Other than the celebration meetings of Ambedkar, it organises meetings to politicise Dalit students. It confines itself to activities related only to the Dalit community. Ideologically, it defines its position assimilating *Marxism* with Ambedkarism for the liberation of Dalits. The campus witnessed the confrontation of Dalit students of PSF and ASA on many isolated incidents. More than ideological fights, the conflict was to establish its organisational hold on campus. On many occasions, both worked together also. In later days, PSF was slowly disappearing and the individuals of the earlier active members of PSF remained to mediate various Dalit and women groups in crucial times. Whatever the anti Dalit attitude shown by the students of upper caste at PSF were now turned against ASA.

Within Andhra Pradesh, there emerged the *Madiga Dandora*, a movement which demanded the categorisation of SC reservations between Dalit sub-castes, Madigas, along with some other smaller castes as Madigas, are relatively deprived in accessing the benefits of SC reservations. All over the state, there emerged a phenomenon of separate Madiga organisations. In the university of Hyderabad also, the numerically small Madiga community had gone away from ASA and formed themselves into a separate organisation named Dalit Students union (DSU). This organisation has been facing problems due to its numerically less number. ASA remained predominantly a Mala organisation. Due to mutual hostilities, these communities could not engage in any negotiations with each other. These communities always organised themselves with reference to other community. DSU too organised along the same lines as ASA. But the difference was that it involved Madiga leaders and employees. If ASA was supporting one group, DSU used to support another group in the students' elections by bargaining for one small post like the cultural secretary or joint secretary.

There has always been a stereotype created of Dalits by the upper castes. This time, the round had come to ASA. ASA has made attempts to take part in the various activities of the university or to actively participate in the affairs of the university. For instance, they wanted to participate as mess secretaries in hostel messes. They want to participate in orchestra by dancing. They were otherwise left out of all the programmes. They wanted to make their presence more visible. When they participated as mess secretaries, they were projected as corrupt. Any body can be corrupt, but projecting it as the character of the community lead to a situation of hostility and confrontation. When they participated in the university functions like orchestra, they were projected as troublemakers and creators of terror. There are other stereotypes in circulation as scholarship holders swallowing govt. money etc. They are also portrayed as violent people. These stereotypes cannot be changed without public articulation. The major problem of the campus Dalit politics is that when one articulates the problem of Dalits in public they are bound to be stereotyped, ridiculed and made to be defeated in a deeply entrenched casteist society. There was no other possible way to convince the public except to thrash and scold out of hopelessness and bitterness. This is again branded as violence and the entire community is depicted as violent. It appears that there is no possibility of going beyond this in the near future. It needs a deep politicisation from both sides. For Dalits, language (English skills) and sophistication is always a problem to express themselves for their genuine justified positions in the public space of university.

The upper caste students do not need any organisation or agitation since their interests are always safeguarded by the university system. The nexus between students-teachers-administration of upper caste is very strong. The whole system is totally dominated by them. So, their interests are taken care of by this dominant system. They project themselves as 'against politics' and 'only for academics'. The imagined threat from the Dalit students too is not ruled out. After the AMCF, there was no organisation formed for upper caste students, though spontaneously they responded in many issues in the name of 'students'. In late nineties, there were efforts from the upper castes to start organisations. 'Discovery' and 'Bermuda' are such organisations and which later formed as ABVP. Both 'Discovery' and 'Bermuda' doesn't have any formal structures. They propagate and circulate stereotypes about Dalits and women through secret posters. Especially the 'Bermuda' publishes secret, vulgar posters particularly aimed at womens' activities. These stereotypes are actively propagated in their informal conversations. They never come in public. But 'Discovery' group organises public seminars with figures like *Arun Shourie*, Gurumurthy of Swadeshi Jagaran Munch etc. Discovery has also been organising RSS sakhas in campus. These two groups are active mobilisers and leaders whenever there is a procession against Dalits. They used to mobilise upper caste vote and also played a crucial role in choosing candidates from the upper caste side. They have also developed a strategy to place Dalit, Muslim or women candidates loyal to the Hindutva ideology to nullify the claims of these actual groups articulating on behalf of them. With the Hindutva forces in power, they created an atmosphere to formally begin a branch of the pro-Hindutva, upper caste ABVP in campus. Both upper caste students and the administration had by then picked up courage to confront and negate Dalit students on campus. This happened in the early years of this decade.

Apart from this, university Discussion Forum (UDF), a liberal upper caste organisation, with leanings towards the CPI (M) is active on campus and had managed to win the students union elections. Though progressive, its strength lies in deliberately keeping away from ASA, otherwise it will lose its upper caste base.

On 13th January 2002, ten Dalit research scholars of ASA were rusticated from university of Hyderabad for allegedly beating the chief warden and another warden. The rustication of students was unprecedented either in this university or any other universities of the country. This has once again shown the vulnerable situation of Dalits even in a modern liberal institution like the university. This has invited protests from Dalits and other democratic forces all over the country. This incident is a culminating point for Dalit politics over a period of a decade in the University of Hyderabad. It provides an occasion to retrospectively look at the complex and torturous journey of Dalit politics spanning over more than a decade in an elite university.

In course of time, the campus is aligned in the lines of United Democratic Alliance (ASA, DSU, Women's Collective, United Students Forum, collectively known as UDA, UDF and ABVP at the time of the students' union general elections of 2005. UDF panel got elected over UDA and marginalised ABVP. The successive defeats of ABVP made them to install the portrait of Vivekananda in hostels (as a propaganda measure), which became a point of controversy. ABVP justified this as an honour to a national youth leader. The other organisations UDA and UDF oppose this as an issue of ABVP's effort to communalisation of campus. *Vivekanada* was considered as a symbol of Hindutva appropriated by Hindu communal forces. ASA has taken a stand that *Vivekananda* should be opposed as a Brahminical ideologue who supported the caste system. The under current of struggle over symbols is an act of political assertion of social groups of the campus. The

ABVP poses a question logically, when the portrait of Ambedkar is allowed, why not *Vivekananda*? All these reflect the struggles at a symbolic level between the students of progressive, lower caste and upper castes.

The entry of the Dalits into the space of the University not just built a more creative space within the political atmosphere of the University. It has actually reshaped the intellectual output from the Social Sciences and Humanities departments. Though the upper caste teachers/scholars repeatedly blame the Dalits for "bringing down" the academic standards, the truth is that, the insistent intellectual questioning by Dalit scholars have actually redefined these very disciplines. University of Hyderabad, in that sense, is a pioneering institution that has created many ground breaking dissertations from the nascent Dalit scholarship. It has been quite a fertile ground for production of a thriving Dalit intelligentia, both women and men who are still actively contributing to the literary, cultural, and scholarly fields. The university students and alumni very often provide the political leadership for Dalit struggles in AP.

Negotiating Caste and Gender

To build up the broad based struggles for any democratic society, one has to consider the problems within and with its alliance partners. In the *Dalit movement*, there are various strategies worked out either to achieve political space or to struggle against exploitation. In this direction, Dalits have negotiated with womens' groups, left parties, backward caste groups, tribals and Muslims. In some issues, they had succeeded and on some issues they had failed to reach a common conscience. Besides this, within the Dalit communities, to reach out the common understanding is also identified as a problem. I feel this needs elaborate explanation and following section focuses on this.

The decade of the eighties, India witnessed the emergence of a strong identity politics. The *Dalit movement* and the women's movement emerged as the struggles of a series of identity politics. The debate in the *civil society* influenced the politics of Andhra Pradesh in a significant way. In the name of identity politics, they are sharing the same theoretical platform to assert their identity. Where as the *Dalit movement* brought the issue of caste and its oppression, women's movement brought the issue of gender and its oppression. Both of them are a critique of the liberal politics of the 'universal man' and to a certain extent, with the politics of class struggles. At least in Andhra, both the movements have understanding in countering the ideology of left struggles. Both the struggles succeeded in establishing their own philosophical position and in taking their struggles further. The struggles generated a good amount of literature.

The conscious Dalits considers that women, too, are the oppressed people and victims of the same upper caste Hindu ideology which is patriarchal in nature. So the Dalit groups considered women too to be 'Dalit'. The conscious upper caste women of the womens' groups too extended their support for the struggles of Dalits. From the womens' group of Asmita, writers like Volga and Vasanta Kannabiran endorsed that 'Dalit' connotes conscious people who are struggling against the dominance of caste, religion and patriarchy. The word Dalit came into existence with struggle.[22] It is the symbol of struggle. For the broad based alliance in fighting against the common enemy these kinds of attempts are necessary. In practice, there are conflicts between these in society.

There are questions and confrontations on the issues of womens' reservation, issues of obscenity and rape of women and the question of usage of language in literature. It provides the understanding that 'Dalit' and 'women' are not a homogenous category. As K. Sanjeevi points out, even though they are Dalits, men are always men, and they can never be women and the same applies to women. It is a fact that there exists patriarchy in Dalit men and caste hatred among the non-Dalit women.[23]

Besides their struggles targeting the Hindu social order as a source of oppression for both in different forms, I would like to look into the tensions prevailing among the upper caste women and Dalit men in their everyday life experiences. Further, I would like to extend my argument about how the woman has been used as a moral capital by the upper caste men to counter Dalit political assertion. There is a need to build up the movement to counter the hegemony of the dominant classes/castes by creating the hegemony of the oppressed. This needs a healthy dialogue among the all the oppressed sections of Indian society.

In the context of the increasing claims of Dalits and women (from the upper castes) to gain access to public institutions, the problems are generally posed as a conflict between the two. On the one side, women entering the universities are relatively in a better economical positions compared to men in general and Dalits in particular. They pretend to be 'independent', 'self assertive', 'confident' and are able to 'speak in English. Whereas, Dalits mostly came from rural and very often are the first generation in their families to enter the universities. The cultural environment for the Dalits is new, yet they begin to perceive themselves as assertive because of the influence of ongoing Dalit struggles. They are painted by the others as 'unskilful', 'reservation fellows', 'black', 'ugly', 'non-meritorious' and 'mannerless people'. In the classroom, they are projected as 'dumb', because they are not able to speak in English. There is an attack silently going on psychologically. There is a general hatred towards the Dalits due to the competition of resources and opportunities. It is generally believed by the upper caste students that the Dalits are grabbing their opportunities without having merit. On the other side, any assertion of Dalits is seen as negative, violent, undemocratic and against the development of the nation. Women from upper castes are not free from these attitudes. In a caste dominated society, any proposal from the lower caste boys to upper caste women have been dubbed as indecent and vulgar and not worth acknowledging. For Dalit men, in the emotional front, the access to upper caste women is socially and culturally restricted. The upper caste women share these prejudices against Dalits. In the large-scale mobilisation of the upper caste students against the Dalits at the time of Mandal agitation upper caste women students have played an active role.

Rural India is in no way different from the university. At most the difference may be in the form. For the upper caste men of the village, Dalit women are easily available and are vulnerable preys. There are everyday sexual harassments and rapes on Dalit women going unnoticed. There is no chance for the Dalit women to protect themselves from the sexual exploitation. The State, and its machinery police and judiciary never pay any serious attention to the issues of violence against Dalit women.

In post-independent India, most of the conflicts between the Dalits and the upper castes, in some way or the other, have been connected to issues of women also. One way or other, Dalit men have asserted in public space by making their visibility. The upper caste women have always felt threatened psychologically that somebody will attack them. While walking at public places she has been made to feel insecure. This somebody may read as the image of a rowdy. It is obvious that their imagination meets the lower caste men. In the popular perceptions that 'rowdies', 'goondas', 'criminals' are essentially drawn from lower castes. This situation coincides with the upper caste women's objections for obscenity in films. The films of the nineties have depicting the aggressive, masculine, subaltern hero (Dalit male) in mass cinema pursuing for fleshy, well-nourished, white-skinned female bodies. These situations have received enormous public condemnation as obscene frames. The middle class, upper caste audience has complained that the theatres are no more a place where decent people can sit.

In contemporary times, Dalits are self-asserting and struggling for their rights. They demand *self-respect* and *dignity* for their life. With the rise in Dalit consciousness they are resisting the dominance and cultural hegemony of the upper castes. The upper caste people are unable to tolerate this kind of situation. They are attacking Dalits both physically and psychologically. In most of the cases, they are justifying their attack that these Dalits are harassing the (their) women. Women become used as a moral capital in settling scores with Dalits. They suddenly change into saviours of women. In the public sphere, especially the press, they circulate these kinds of concerns for women. In fact, these are the people responsible for the oppression of women along with nurturing the ideals of caste system. The classic example for this is Tsundur massacre, where eight Dalits were killed in the year 1991 by the upper caste Reddy community with some other communities' support. In response to this, the Dalits organised rallies and have shown their protest against the upper caste dominance. To counter this, the upper caste people mobilised all the upper castes in the pretext that Dalit activists raped their women. By doing this they not only consolidated their base and mobilised support in their favour. At the same time, they succeeded in minimising the support for the Dalit victims from the progressive non-Dalit sections. The women groups were forced to maintain silence.

The issue of women's reservation bill generated much debate in the realm of politics. There was a serious confrontation between women's groups and Dalit groups. The argument in favour of reservation for women was that though women were half the population of the nation, there was no proper political representation for women in legislative bodies. The bill was proposed in the parliament by one govt. after another. Till now, the bill has not been passed.

There are many reasons for the delay. One of the reasons is consideration of sub-quota for Dalits/OBC in the quota of women's reservation. The Dalit leaders and the leaders from backward communities are stressing for this. They put forward the argument that in the name of women, mostly upper caste women will enter the Parliament. The lower caste women will be marginalised forever. Further, they argued that women are not a homogenous category. They too are divided in terms of caste, religion, class etc. The women's groups and some of the women parliamentarians like Mamata Banerjee countered this argument that political parties are not sincere enough in this issue and are finding strategies to not pass this bill. The women leaders mainly argued that irrespective of caste, patriarchal dominance and exploitation is everywhere. For this, Dalit men are no exception. The feminist leaders, like Vasanta Kannabiran and many other women activists of the country felt that let the women's reservation bill pass in the parliament in existing form. Later, one can discuss about caste (OBC women) and religion (minority women). The leaders who are arguing for the passing for the bill after the incorporation of the sub quota for OBC, Dalit and minority women were branded by the women activists as 'anti-women'. They accused them as not being sincere for the women's cause. Further, these women leaders were shouting to them that all women are same, why do you people create division among us, which are not there. The media too helped them in portraying leaders like Mulayam Singh, Lalu Prasad Yadav and Kanshiram as 'villains' in this whole episode. It is a well shared opinion in media run by the upper caste and middle class that these Dalits are 'fools', 'jokers', can't speak English properly, and doesn't have either skill, or eligibility to rule the nation. Due to these people our Indian politics was blamed to have become corrupt, criminalised, and violent. Their anxieties and aspirations are considered as nonsensical and undemocratic.

One should not forget that these lower caste leaders not only challenged the hegemony of the upper caste in politics, but also gave new meanings to Indian politics. It is a known reality that these leaders have more experience and access to their respective castes than the upper caste women. In a society, where the social relations are defined/ constructed on the basis of caste, it is an uncontested truth that people (women) within the caste will speak wholeheartedly than with upper caste women coming from the cities. It doesn't mean that there is no dialogue between Dalit women and conscious urban upper caste women.

Dalit women are victims of both caste dominance and patriarchy along with poverty. Caste dominance relatively plays an important role than patriarchy in the liberation of Dalit women. There is a criticism against the feminist groups that they are urban centred and mostly confined to the problems faced by upper caste women. They don't have to touch the problems of rural women. Particularly, the problems of the Dalit woman are quite different from the urban upper caste woman's problems. By realising this, organisations of women in affiliation to the revolutionary parties got activated. Anti-arrack struggles of women is one such example in this context.

Politically conscious groups of Dalits and women are mutually sensitive to the concerned issues. They understand that the contradiction between the two are delicate and need creative intervention. There are occasions in Andhra, where both have supported each other by correcting their positions. They treat the contradiction between them as a friendly contradiction. I would like to mention two such occasions, one is in literary debate and other the women's reservation issue in the University of Hyderabad.

I feel it worth considering the struggles relating to the issue of women's reservation in the students' union of the university of Hyderabad in the year 1999, in the backdrop of the controversy of women's representation bill. The active negotiation of women's invisibility in student electoral politics underwent a radical transformation when issues of caste were addressed simultaneously with those of gender. With the consistent pressure of women's group on campus, the general body meeting was announced to discus the amendment of the students' union constitution. A few Dalit women immediately raised the issue of representation of Dalit women in the students' union. A representative post for women that didn't take into account the differences between women (specifically between Dalit women and upper caste women) was as guilty of practices of exclusion as the students' union had for the last twenty five years. The difference here with the parliament is that Dalit women were making the claim for themselves. This situation has the implications for both women's organisations and Dalit organisations of the campus. 'The women's movement, that has been largely upper caste, and the Dalit movement that has been largely male, will both be forced to listen, will both have to re-examine their agendas, revise them and negotiate space for the Dalit women.'[24]

With the forceful entry of Dalit women, the demand changed to women's representation on a rotational basis for one post in the union. Interestingly, the upper caste women who were predominant in the movement had been distinctly uncomfortable with the word 'reservation' and were willing to discuss the same as 'the special problems' faced by women. At the same time, the moment Dalit women and men became active participants in the struggle, the word reservation became imbued with new meanings–it came to signify a history of struggles and became a word to be used with pride. On these issues the joint action committee was formed of all progressive, Dalit and women's organisations to negotiate this issue further. The student's union had been willing to discuss the gender question in its initial GBM, as soon as the issue of caste came up with a post on rotational basis, it refused to take it seriously. 'This alliance between Dalit women, upper caste women, Dalit men and progressive upper caste men was remarkable also because it offered possibilities that were different from those before parliament today.'[25]

The other groups who were resisting women's reservation were upper caste and pro-Hindu groups. They continued their alliances. As expected, reservations for women didn't get the requisite two-third majority to force an amendment of the student's union's constitution. At the same time, the upper castes and Hindutva organisations who voted for outright denial of women reservation too failed to get the two third majority to oppose it. It was a moral victory for the joint action committee of women, Dalit and progressive forces who consolidated their identity by opposing the upper caste men's stand in this issue. This provides an example of an active alliance of forces of Dalit men, women and other progressive groups in negotiating for social justice. At the same time, it reveals the problems within and to think of the strategies to be adopted to realise their agendas.

Another issue that is taken up to show the possibilities of a gender caste negotiation is a controversy raised in the Telugu literary circles. The feminist writers objected to the words of slang used by the Dalit writers and asked them to correct. They appealed to the Dalit writers who were struggling for the liberation of Dalits to reform their language, since most of the slang or obscene words in circulation are targeted against women. They are centred on the body parts of women. They were words of insult to women. They, too, agreed that when their women are raped and sexually humiliated by upper caste men, the anger of Dalit men can be understood. Let the Dalit women speak how to retaliate to such situations. They cautioned the male Dalit writers to think about the words used by them like-'we will rape your mothers and sisters'. As the feminist writers said, to take revenge in religious and caste conflicts through the bodies of women which are using as an instrument is an old technique. In the liberation struggles if women are seen as instruments of revenge, than the individual, then what meaning we are giving for the liberation struggle? Can't we think about other alternative than imitating the language of the enemy. We can't win the battle with owner by using the tools of owner.[26]

In Telugu literature, the feminist writers conceptualised the body politics in their writings. Female body is identified as a site of oppression. They countered the patriarchal constructions of women bodies. From feudal times, till today, men controlled the women through the ideology of patriarchy. To sustain its rule, the Hindu social order played a vital role. The philosophies and religious doctrines contributed for the subordination of women and allowed the hegemony of male dominance. Patriarchy got strengthened in its foundation by continuing the caste system. Ambedkar realised very earlier that patriarchal system is inseparable relation with *caste system*. The freedom of the women, status of women in family and civil society is directly linked with the Hindu caste system. This caste is sustained through the maintenance of hierarchy and the principles of endogamy. This endogamy rules out any interaction and intermarriage with the other castes. Ambedkar had foreseen that women were centrally located in the struggle against the caste system. He proposed the Hindu code bill in the parliament for the codification of laws in empowering women socially and economically.[27] The Hindu code bill discussed the Hindu marriage act, divorce and inheritance of property rights for the benefit of women. This bill is opposed by majoritarian caste Hindus. There is no difference after fifty years of this episode. But the upper caste Hindus succeeded in putting the women to counter the Dalits. This can be seen in the case of women's reservation issue and Tsundur massacre issue. The Hindu upper castes picked up the liberal language (contrary to its spirit) to negate the claims of Dalits.

At the same time there were attempts to come together by the conscious sections of Dalits, women and progressive groups. This can be seen in the case of struggles of women's representation in the students' union of the university and mutual reciprocation of feminist and Dalit writers against the common enemy. In this effort either women or Dalits should maintain exclusiveness in articulating their problems and political position and at the same time should maintain inclusiveness of all progressive groups in building the struggles against oppression and hegemony of dominant castes and classes.

Dalit Politics and the Sub-Caste Issue

There are many studies in understanding Dalit movement from relative deprivation point of view. This relative deprivation theory holds very well in understanding the urban Dalits in relation to the upper castes at a vertical level. Dalits feel relatively deprived both socially and materially in comparison with the upwardly mobile upper castes. The reference group is this upwardly mobile upper castes. To overcome this kind of deprivation they demand more patronage from the system. Whereas the upper castes successfully marginalise both in everyday *civil society* in the name of 'efficiency' and 'merit'. They project the Dalit class as a hurdle for development and brand them as corrupt.

In the awakening of Dalit consciousness, there are inevitable inherent problems within Dalit communities. The word Dalit is an umbrella term to bring many oppressed communities under this. This political category makes a constant effort in uniting many communities at the cost of minimising the differences. This consolidation may help in countering the hegemony of the dominant caste groups. History reveals that there is an inbuilt hatred among the Dalit communities and this may damage any initiative at the consolidation of Dalit masses. This needs proper historical explanation on why there is more violence in horizontal plane than vertical plane. Here too, many communities try to articulate from the relative deprivation point of view. The prominent examples to explain this is, the conflict between Dalits sub castes, the Malas and the Madigas in Andhra Pradesh, the Mangs and the Mahars in Maharashtra, the the Holeyas and the Aurundhatiyas in Karnataka, the Pallars and the Paraiahs in Tamil Nadu etc.

To bring all the sub-castes of the Dalit community together is a difficult task. Even Ambedkar faced difficulties in bringing all the Dalit sub-caste groups as a consolidated force during his lifetime. One may be surprised to see that there is a gulf between the different lower caste groups. On the one hand, Dalit communities are discriminated by the upper caste groups. On the other hand, amongst the subcaste groups there are no marriages and inter-dining practices. However, this doesn't mean that Dalit solidarity is impossible. With the rising political consciousness among all its sub castes, there are serious attempts to mobilise the Dalit communities against the common enemy-caste Hindu hegemonic forces. There is no doubt that the *Dalit movement* has politicised all the lower caste groups. The word 'Dalit' worked as a class-like term. Like class formation which brings people sharing the same class from diverse social and cultural backgrounds, 'Dalit' too functioned as a common identity for many sub-castes groups of lower castes despite the differences among themselves. The common political aspiration is binding on them.

The *Dalit movement* came into existence not only through its struggles against the exploitation of caste Hindus, but also raised the voice against the dominance of one Dalit sub-caste against the other. In other words, Dalit consciousness helped in asserting the identity of every Dalit sub-caste. There is a criticism that independent and autonomous assertion of each sub-caste may liquidate the consolidation of Dalit solidarity. This may be helpful to the ruling upper caste groups. Some argue that the creation of divisions among Dalit sub castes is a conscious effort of the ruling Brahminical forces. In response to it, others argue that this may strengthen the *Dalit movement* by realising one's own self instead of weakening the *Dalit movement*. First of all, one should be realistic and open in understanding the internal contradictions among the Dalit sub castes. There is a need to address the internal differences 'within' the Dalit sub castes simultaneously with the struggles against the upper caste hegemony. However, mostly the differences among Dalit sub castes surfaced in sharing opportunities, material benefits, and resources in the public sector and in the issues of political representation. In the nineties, the political development of the *Dalit movement* of Andhra explains this. The emergence of Madiga *Dandora movement*, is a movement of the Madiga sub-caste assertion. It demanded categorisation of reservation as per population. This brings out the problems involved in Dalit consolidation.

In Andhra Pradesh, Mala and Madiga are numerically strong sub caste out of 59 Dalit sub castes. The Mala community does not have any traditional occupation. They are a relatively free and mobile community mostly located in coastal Andhra. Whereas, the Madiga community, historically, has taken up cobbling as a their caste profession. They are mostly located in Telangana and some pockets of coastal Andhra and Rayalaseema region. However, both are poor agricultural labourers and are treated badly by the upper caste Hindus. While in the 1985 Karamchedu massacre, Dalits belonging to the Madiga community were killed by the upper caste Kamma landlords, in the 1991 Tsunduru massacre, the Dalits of the Mala community were killed by the upper castes of the Reddy community. In the Vempenta episode, the Madigas of Rayalseema were burnt to ashes.

Though there are difference among these two communities, they have worked together in the Dalit movement. With the *Karamchedu issue*, the *Dalit Mahasabha* formed itself and both the communities had identified with it.

In July 7,1994 *Madiga Reservation Porata Samithi* (MRPS) was formed and demanded further categorisation of the existing 15% reservations for SCs. They argued for this on the basis of the fact that Madigas were deprived of the benefits of reservations. It further pointed out that more than 80 per cent of reservations were enjoyed by the Mala sub-caste. So, it demanded that the Government should take measures so that the benefits of reservation would reach all the sub castes as per population. The Telugu Desam Party Government formed the Justice Ramachandra Raju commission to look into the issue. The ordinance later became an Act in May 2, 2000. Today, SC reservation is divided into 1:7:6:1 for A, B, C, D groups respectively. A group comprises of Relli sub castes, B consists Madiga subcastes, C group Mala subcastes and D group Adi-andhra subcaste. Against this move the Mala subcaste group formed the *Mala Mahanadu* in June 6, 2000. Mala Mahanadu argues that the categorisation of Scheduled castes will divide the Dalit community and there is a need to fight unitedly against the exploiting upper-caste groups. One more argument put forwarded by the Malas that there are equal opportunities for both. Madigas countered this argument by saying it was in tune with upper-caste merit argument. The conflict amongst these two sub castes focussed primarily on material benefits. This issue created misunderstanding and suspicion between both the Dalit communities. A vertical divide seem to separate these two Dalit communities with one group supporting the Telugu Desam party and other the *Congress party* in the last General Elections (2004).

Against the G.O. of S.C. categorisation, Mala Mahanadu appealed to the Supreme Court and got a verdict in its favour. In its judgment, Supreme Court mentions that state government doesn't have the authority to categorise scheduled castes. Only the Parliament is invested with the power to further categorise. In its judgement, it considers Scheduled castes as a class.

Ambedkar too faced difficulty in consolidating the Dalit sub castes in his times for a common cause. There is a strong opinion that sub caste consciousness leads to the disintegration of the *Dalit movement*. But history reveals that there are many struggles fought by the Dalit sub castes collectively against their common enemy. The Karamchedu struggle is classic example to this. It has to be understood that without addressing the specificity and problems of ones own sub castes, it is difficult to build a common Dalit struggle. As *Franz Fanon* in the context of blacks argues that there is much violence in horizontal line than vertical line. This may hold true in case of Dalits too that their anger reflected on the people of same plane than the dominant exploited castes. Limitation of energies of Dalits in terms of political and economical may be one the reasons for this.

Politics of Hindu Nationalism: A Challenge to Secular State (Dalits, Women, and Minorities etc.)

In contemporary times, religious nationalism emerged as global phenomenon. There are many struggles rallying around this ideology. This phenomenon coincides with the changing economic scenario of the world. There is a disorder in the lives of people and the world. The people and the world lost direction. Both the ideals of American capitalist economic model and Russian socialist models are no more inspiring. After the disintegration of the Soviet Union, it appears that America managed to become a super power. It is apt to say that the contemporary world is multi polar rather than unipolar. There is a serious competition among the developed nations in terms of trade and monopoly of global capital and the developing and under developed nations got blow with the adaptation of new economic policies. Globalisation has distorted the lives and values of the third world. Political uncertainty witnessed the entrenchment of corrupt governments. Mostly the third world nations got released from the *colonialism* in the decade of fifties and got involved in the building the nation. The ideals for the foundation of nation is '*Secularism*', '*modernity*', 'progress', 'development' are at a stake at the contemporary times. The way it is carried over the nation are questioned by some scholars. There is a serious rethinking on the issue of imagination of the nation state with changing aspirations of the various social groups of the nation. As a solution for the real problems in a crisis ridden society people started relying on religion/ God. The solution for the problems of this world is finding in the other world. There is a heavy investment to selective invention of the past to build the nation from all the social groups. In

India, nation building can be seen simultaneously from upper caste Hindu middle classes and lower caste groups. The upper caste Hindu middle classes imagination of the nation in the name of *Hindu nationalism* has taken edge over others as the genuine and natural. The social and cultural capital of these classes helped to establish this dominance over other social communities. At present, the Hindu nationalists are confronting the existing secular State in all possible ways In the name of protecting the nation/culture/religion from the other, they are protecting/consolidating their social position in the wake of democratic struggles of the other oppressed communities of the nation. For this purpose they are selective in targeting the Indian Muslims by portraying them as potential enemies to the integration of nation.

Hindu Nationalists and Indian Upper Caste/Middle Class

In late eighties, the politics of militant *Hindu nationalism* came to forefront with the rise of Hindu upper caste middle class with fulfilment of their social aspiration. The secret of success of these groups lies in bringing the two strong emotional identities together, namely 'religion' and 'nation'. Both of these identities are strongly rooted in the past. It is easy to invoke the feelings of belongingness, our culture, our nation, our religion in a crisis ridden uncertain situation. Because of the given advantage this upper caste Hindu middle castes naturally appropriate the legacy of progressive struggles of the past. They will pose as real inheritors of the cultural ideals that are established by the people with lots of sacrifice. These groups project themselves as the protectors of the nation by labeling others as enemies of the nation. The Hindu nationalists are campaigning constantly that Indian Muslims are 'other', 'foreigners' and 'not loyal to nation'. In the name of Hindu majoritarian rule they are deliberate enough to keep out the minority Muslims. These social elite are tactful in cementing through the *Hindu nationalism*, the differences within *Hinduism*. One has to understand this in the context where Dalits, adivasis, Backward caste groups, the victims of the caste system are struggling against caste oppression and are keeping away from the Hindu fold.

One has to note that this same upper caste Hindu middle class have anger and hatred against the lower caste groups who are taking away their opportunities through reservations. These classes are bringing the argument of 'merit', 'hard work' and 'efficiency' to counter the reservations and the lower caste groups. The interesting turning point is that there is a serious competition for the resources and opportunities. Strong feeling among them is that Dalits and women are grabbing their opportunities through reservations. They have therefore suddenly shifted to reservations based on economic position, hatred against them justified in the name of 'efficiency', 'hard work', 'merit'.

These people are very much aware of the problems involved in directly targeting the lower castes. The struggles of the lower caste have moral and political potential to expose the wrong doings of the upper caste by taking the same history. The upper caste Hindu middle castes in India succeeded in their effort to push their aspiration at the cost of demonising Muslims. By targeting the Muslims they walked over the Dalits, women and other marginalised people of India.

Debate of Secularism/Pseudo-Secularism

In India, secularism had taken roots as an ideal of liberal democracy. Broadly, the ideology of secularism considers state to play neutral role in the affairs of religion. It should not discriminate, or support any religion.It is considered as an ideal to be followed in a nation like ours where many religions and social groups exist. In recent times, the debate on *secularism* has received currency. The leaders and scholars, who are supporters of democratic struggles of the nation, are critical about the *Hindu nationalists* for their confrontation with *secular* state. The *Hindu nationalists* responded to their criticism by calling them 'pseudo-secularists' and claiming themselves as true secularists. They are arguing that 'tolerance' is the very cultural ideal of *Hinduism* from time immemorial. Interestingly, one can see the redefining of *secularism* by the *Hindu nationalist*. The language of *liberal* politics is moulded for their convenience. It can be seen that Hindu nationalists, whenever the lower caste groups or women demand their rights in an unequal Indian society, these groups pick up the language that everybody should be treated equal. There should not be any concession, or reservations based on caste, religion, or gender.

Towards the Democratisation of Indian Society

Secularism should not be mistaken for discrimination against religion. In fact, most of the debate is centred on cultural issues. One should not forget that culture is an epiphenomenon of social and economic development of society. It is a social expression.

The *Hindu nationalists* have not extended their debate on *secularism* to social and economic spheres. They are limited to the cultural sphere. Their struggles got attention by provoking the feelings of 'belongingness,' 'our culture,' and 'our nation.' They never bothered against the economic reforms that are responsible for the present situation. They welcome the multinationals companies, they dream about landing in USA. They are confident enough that the lower castes may not enter this arena.

Indian politics is emotionally manipulated by the nationalistic claims of the Hindutva forces. Any struggle against the Hindutva forces is dubbed as anti national. They are consciously propagating this through their middle class machinery. In the name of the Indian nation and Indian culture they are attracting all the social groups including Dalits and Adivasis. This coincides with the people's experience of threat of loss of culture and collective life in the wake of globalisation. But the nationalism propagated by the *Hindutva* forces is confined to cultural nationalism in a selective way, but not connected to economic and social development. Cultural nationalism has no meaning unless until it is connected to social *equality* and *social justice*. It is clear that in the scheme of the upper caste Indian nationalism (Hindu nationalism), social aspirations and imaginations of Dalits, women and Adivasis have got marginalised. As *Benedict Anderson* argues the nation is nothing but the imagination of a community. Taking clue from this *Partha Chatterjee* explains that the building of the Indian nation takes place simultaneously from the social aspirations and anxieties of upper caste, middle class from the above and marginalised lower castes from below. After all, any nation comes into existence with its struggles. History of the people cannot be manipulated forever. With the intense struggles of the Dalits and other marginalised communities, a more democratic nation will come into existence. In this sense the Dalit Indian nationalism is different from the Indian nation aspired by the social groups belonging to the upper castes. In building this one can explore the political philosophy of Ambedkar who is rooted in the indigenous tradition. He too proposes a religious nationalism, which is not dogmatic and irrational but critical about traditions and democratic in its functioning.

In conclusion, we identified the limitations of Ambedkar's framework as well as the relevance of Ambedkar's ideology in the post-independent period. To address the new challenges of contemporary times, the situation demands the creative reinterpretation of Ambedkar. For this, dalit struggles have to go beyond symbolic identification with Ambedkar.

Notes

1. Kesava Kumar. P., Jiddu Krishna murti's Conception of Tradition and Revolution : A Critical Study, Ph.D dissertation submitted to University of Hyderabad, 1997. p. 232.
2. Alam, Javeed, India: Living with Modernity, Oxford University Press, Delhi, 1999, p. 4.
3. Duing the budget debates on electricity projects in the Madras Legislative Council in 1936, lower caste representatives constantly asked for appointment of lower caste people in the Department of Electricity.
4. Ramulu, P.C., "Gayam Kotthakadu." (The Wound is not New) In Kesava Kumar & K. Satyanarayana (Eds.) Dalit Manifesto, Hyderabad: Vishphotana, 1995.
5. Prasad, Kalekuri, "Pidikedu Atmagauravam Kosam Talettina Vadini," (Am Raised for a Fistful of Self-respect), In Kesava Kumar & K. Satyanarayana (Eds.) Dalit Manifesto, Hyderabad: Vishphotana, 1995.
6. Ambedkar, B.R., Dr. Babasaheb Ambedkar Writings and Speeches, Vol. 9. Mumbai: Education Department, Government of Maharashtra, 1991, pp. 42-52.
7. *Ibid*, Vol. 9, pp. 70-71.
8. Das, Bhagawan, "Moments in the History of Reservations." The Economic and Political Weekly, October 28, 2000, p. 38.
9. Guru, Gopal, "Dr.Ambedkar's Concept of Political Power and the Question of Dalit Movement" In Dr. Ambedkar Memorial Lecture, Hyderabad: Ambedkar Memorial Trust, 1993, p. 37.
10. *Ibid*, p. 370.

11. *Ibid*, p. 38.
12. *Ibid*, p. 52.
13. Omvedt, Gail, "Kanshiram and the Bahujan Samaj Party". In K. L. Sharma (ed.) Caste and Class in India, New Delhi: Rawat Publications, 1998, p. 157.
14. Laxmi Narasaiah, G. and Tripuraneni Sreenivas (Eds.) Chikkanavutunna Pata (Thickening Song), Vijayawada: Kavitvam, 1995.
15. Kesava Kumar and K. Satyanarayana (Eds.) Dalit Manifesto, Hyderabad: Vishpotana, 1995.
16. Laxminarasaih, G. (Ed.) Padunekkina Pata (Sharpened Song), Vijayawada: Dalita Sana, 1996.
17. Satyanarayana, K. Eee Potee Venaka Vunnadi Kutra, *Andhrajothy Daily*, Sunday, January 28, 1996.
18. Laxminarasaiah, G. Dalit Sahityanikee Viplava Sahityanikee Ddrukpadhallo Tedavundi, *Andhrajyothy Sunday*, December 17, 1995.
19. Je. Sree, Potee Anadam Vidduram -Kutra Anadam Kruram, *Andhrajyothy Daily*, Sunday, February 18, 1996.
20. *Danee, Usha S.*, Mudu Sangha Samskaranalu-Aru Dalita Srenulu, *Andhrajothy Daily*, Sunday, August 13, 1995.
21. Kalyana Rao, G. Antarani Vasantham (Untouchable Spring), Hyderabad: Virasam, 2000.
22. Volga,Vasanta Kannabhiran and Kalpana Kannbhiran, "Yejamani Audhalatho Yejamani Soudhanni Kulagottagalama", In S.V. Satyanarayana, (Ed.) Dalitavada Vivadalu, Hyderabad: Visalandhra Publishing House, 1999, p. 115.
23. Sanjeevi, K., Nirdishatanundi Anirdhisthataku, In S.V. Satanarayana (Ed.) Dalitavad Vivadalu, Dalitavada Vivadalu, Hyderabad : Visalandhra Publishing House, 1999, p. 147.
24. Joint Action Committee (JAC), Negotiating Gender and Caste, *The Economic and Political Weekly*, October 28, 2000, pp. 3846.
25. *Ibid*, p. 3847.
26. Volga,Vasanta Kannabhiran and Kalpana Kannbhiran, "Yejamani Audhalatho Yejamani Soudhanni Kulagottagalama" In S.V. Satyanarayana (Ed.) Dalitavada Vivadalu, Hyderabad: Visalandhra Publishing House, 1999, p. 119.
27. See Shonalkar, Vandana, "An Agenda for Gender Politics," *The Economic and Political Weekly*, Januaury 2-5, 1999.

Conclusion

Ambedkar is the source for alternative social movements. The very fact that his thought has become a point of intense debate to all streams of politics itself indicates his importance to any project of emancipation in India. Especially, it is difficult to see the *Dalit movement* as detached from Ambedkar. Ambedkar acts as both a symbolic and an ideological force for the Dalits of contemporary India. Though the Dalit movement seems to have discontinuity with the basic premises of Ambedkar, there is a lot of similarity in terms of substance. The discontinuity is due to long journey that Dalits have taken to post independent India. Dalit assertion has taken diverse forms in different places because of presence of different communities among the Dalits, nature of socio-economic development and local cultural traditions. Different cultural traditions gives rise to different kinds of dissent, hence it is too naïve to look for Ambedkarism in itself in every Dalit protest.

Ambedkar provides a method to understand *Indian philosophy*. He came up with novel philosophical position by interrogating the dominant philosophical traditions of India. His notion of philosophy is close to social experiences of suffering masses. For him, philosophy is the social expression that looks for liberation. Unlike the dominant Indian philosophical traditions; his political thought is rational rather than speculative. This allows Dalit movement to engage critically with any social, cultural and political issues. Ambedkar offers critical tools in interrogating traditions of dominant groups and also he felt the necessity to create critical, rational and democratic traditions of oppressed communities.

Ambedkar is critical about religion from a philosophical perspective and looks for a moral community. His conception of community is very novel. His moral community has based on the principles of *equality*, *liberty* and fraternity. He defends the community for enlarging the space of freedom and equality. He demands individual freedom, when the individual was a victim of dominant community and argues for democratic community as against the individual. He connects the individual and community based on morality. He does not confirm to either Hindu ideal community or Marxist conception of community based on participation in production process. His conception of community is moral and ethical. It is not automatically available for participation in common affairs. His idea of community has to be created through hard and torturous process of moral transformation. When Ambedkar criticises Hindu community for its oppressive nature, he does it with a standard of individual liberty and freedom. When he is talking about suffering of individual members of Dalit community he is projecting an ideal model community based on *equality*, *liberty* and *fraternity*. So it is not correct to call Ambedkar as either a fierce individualist or as a strong communitarian. However, Ambedkar's philosophy has a potential to mediate both *liberalism* and *communitarianism* from the non-western context.

Ambedkar is not a dogmatist who follows one particular strategy throughout his life time. He transforms himself many times in his life by actively participating in politics and reflection. As some commentators have pointed out there are many phases in his life. He leans towards liberals at some point of time, and Marxists at some other point in time depending on the nature of issue at hand. Because of this strategy, he has variety of positions on State, economy, class, dominant caste Hindus, Hindu religion etc. *Dalit Movement* has its own positions. It is important to study Ambedkar's positions and appropriate them critically and creatively for the purpose of Dalit emancipation.

The political philosophy of Ambedkar may help in renegotiating the crisis of western political theory in particular and leading the struggles of the masses in general. In assessing the political philosophy of Ambedkar, the existing language of political traditions is not enough to capture his thought. It does not mean that his philosophy has an affinity and difference with the liberal, conservative and radical characterisation of existing political traditions. This pragmatic approach is an innovative contribution to Indian political theory and practice. The essence of his pragmatism is to make Dalits, a center of any emancipatory project.

Bibliography

Agarwal, Pratab Chandra, Halfway to Equality, Delhi: Manohar, 1983.

Agarwal, Sudharsham (ed.), *Dr. B.R., Ambedkar -The Man and his Message: A Commemorative volume*, Delhi: Prentice Hall of India Pvt. Ltd., 1991.

Ahmed, Aizaz, "The Politics of State", *Frontline*, February 12, 1999.

Alam, Javeed, "Is Caste Appeal Casteism? Oppressed Castes in Politics" *Economic and Political Weekly*, March 27, 1999, pp. 757 -761

Alam, Javeed, *India Living with Modernity*, New Delhi:Oxford University Press, 1999.

Aloysius, G. *Dalit-Subaltern Emergence in Religio-Cultural Subjectivity; Iyothee Thassar and Emancipatory Budhism*, New Delhi: Critical Quest, 2004.

Ambedkar and Social Justice (Vol. 1.), New Delhi: Ministry of Information and Broad Casting, 1992.

Ambedkar and Social Justice (Vol. 2.), New Delhi: Ministry of Information and Broadcasting, 1992.

Ambedkar, B.R., *Dr. Babasaheb Ambedkar Writings and Speeches, Vol. 1*, Mumbai: Education Department, Governement of Maharashtra, 1989.

Ambedkar, B.R., *Dr. Babasaheb Ambedkar Writings and Speeches, Vol. 2*, Mumbai: Education Department, Government of Maharashtra, 1982.

Ambedkar, B.R., *Dr. Babasaheb Ambedkar Writings and Speeches, Vol. 3*, Mumbai: Education Department, Government of Maharashtra, 1987.

Ambedkar, B.R., *Dr. Babasaheb Ambedkar Writings and Speeches, Vol. 4*, Mumbai: Education Department, Government of Maharashtra, 1987.

Ambedkar, B.R., *Dr. Babasaheb Ambedkar Writings and Speeches, Vol. 5*, Mumbai: Education Department, Government of Maharashtra, 1989.

Ambedkar, B.R., *Dr. Babasaheb Ambedkar Writings and Speeches, Vol. 6*, Mumbai: Education Department, Government of Maharashtra, 1989.

Ambedkar, B.R., *Dr. Babasaheb Ambedkar Writings and Speeches, Vol. 7*, Mumbai: Education Department, Government of Maharashtra, 1990.

Ambedkar, B.R., *Dr. Babasaheb Ambedkar Writings and Speeches, Vol. 8*, Mumbai: Education Department, Government of Maharashtra, 1990.

Ambedkar, B.R., *Dr. Babasaheb Ambedkar Writings and Speeches, Vol. 9,* Mumbai: Education Department, Governement of Maharashtra, 1991.

Ambedkar, B.R., *Dr. Babasaheb Ambedkar Writings and Speeches, Vol. 10,* Mumbai: Education Department, Government of Maharashtra, 1991.

Ambedkar, B.R., *Dr. Babasaheb Ambedkar Writings and Speeches, Vol. 11,* Mumbai: Education Department, Government of Maharashtra, 1992.

Ambedkar, B.R., *Dr. Babasaheb Ambedkar Writings and Speeches, Vol. 12,* Mumbai: Education Department, Government of Maharashtra, 1993.

Ambedkar, B.R., *Dr. Babasaheb Ambedkar Writings and Speeches, Vol. 17,* (Part 1, 2 and 3) Mumbai: Education Department, Governement of Maharashtra, 2003.

Anand, Mulk Raj, The Utouchable (Novel), Harmnodsorth : Penguin Books, 1986.

Ananda Rao, K., "Bhuswamya Samskriti Srustinchina Samasye Harijana Samasya". *Prajasahiti Vol. 1, issue 3,* October 1977.

Anandhi, S., Contesting Identifies: Dalits and Secular Politics in Madras Slums, New Delhi: Indian Social Institute, 1995.

Andhra Pradesh Pourahakkula Sangham (Andhra Pradesh Civil Liberties Committe Document) *Dalitulapai Dadulu Agedeppudu?* Hyderabad: APCLC Publications, February, 2002.

Appadorai A., Documents on Political Thought in Modern India, Vol. 1 & 2, Bombay.

Appadorai, A. Indian Political Thinking Through the Ages, New Delhi: Khama Publishers, 1992.

Aravind, P. and V. Devasahayam (Eds.), *Dr. Ambedkar : A Centenary Tribute,* Madras: Gurukul Luthern Theological College and Research Institute, 1991.

Bains, Ravinder Singh, Reservation Policy and Anti-Reservationists, Delhi: B R Publishing Corporation, 1994.

Balagopal K., "Post-Chundur and other Chundurs", *Economic and Political Weekly,* October, 19, 1991.

Balagopal, K., "Marathi-Gujaratee Dalita Sahityam" *Arunatara, March 1982* pp. 4-10.

Baradwaja A N., The Problems of Scheduled Castes and Scheduled Tribes in India, New Delhi: Lights Life Publishers, 1979.

Baxi, Upendra and Bikhu Parekh, Crisis and Change in Contemporary India, New Delhi: Sage, 1995.

Bayle, Susan, Caste, Society and Politics in India, Cambridge University Press: Cambridge, 1999.

Bayly, Susan, Caste, Society and Politics in India; From Eighteenth Century to the Modern Age Cambridge: Cambridge University Press, 2002.

Beteille, Andre, Caste, Class and Power Changing Patterns of Stratification of Tanjore Village, New Delhi: Oxford University Publications, 1996.

Beteille, Andre, The Backward Classes and the New Social Order, New Delhi: Oxford University Press, 1988.

Bharata Desamulo Kula Samasya: Mana Drukpadham (Caste Problem in India: Our Point of View) CPI (ML) People's War Document, 1996.

Bharill, Chandra Social and Political Ideas of B.R., Ambedkar, Jaipur: Rawat Publications, 1977.

Bose, Sugata & Ayesha Jalal (ed.), Nationalism, Democracy and Development State.

Bowes, Pratima, "What is Indian about Indian Philosophy?" S.S. Ramarao Pappu and R. Puligandla (Eds.) Indian Philosophy: Past and Future, New Delhi: Motilal Banarsidas,1982, pp. 3-15.

Bramsted EK & K J Mathur (eds.), Western Liberalism: A History in Documents from

Brass, Paul R., The New Cambridge History of India, The politics of India since

Brigg, G.W., The Chamars, Delhi: Low Price Publications, 1998.

Calhoun, Craig (ed.), Social Theory and the Politics of Identity, Oxford: Blackwell, 1994.

Cambridge University Press, 1985.

Chanchareek (ed). Dr. B.R., Ambedkar 1891 -1991, Vol.1, Fight for the Right of the Depressed Classes, Delhi: H.K. Publishers, 1991.

Chanchreek K.L. (ed.), B.R., Ambedkar, 1899-1991, Patriot, Philosopher and Statesman, New Delhi: H.K. Publishers, 1991.

Chandrasekhar Reddy R., & K. Laxminarayana (eds.), Dalila Kathalu, Hyderabad: Visalandra Publishers, 1996.

Chatterjee, Partha (ed.), State and Politics in India, Delhi: Oxford University Press, 1997.

Chatterjee, Partha, Nation and its Fragments, Delhi: Oxford University Press, 1994.

Chatterjee, Surjit Kumar, Schedule Castes in India (Vol. 4), Delhi: Gyan Publishing House, 1996.

Chinna Rao, Yaganti, Dalit's struggle for Identity: Andhra and Hyderabad, 1900-1950. Delhi: Kanishka, 2003.

Clarke, Satianathan, Dalits and Christianity, Subaltern Religion and Liberation theology in India, Delhi: Oxford University Press, 1998.

CPI (M L) Janasakti Document Kulam Samasya Pai, May 17 Groupki CPI (M L) Janasakthi Samadhanam, Hyderabad : CPI (ML) Janasakti Prachuranalu, January 1999.

Dallmaye, Fred R. (Ed). From Contract to Community, New York: Marcel Dekkar Inc., 1978.

Danee, Usha S, Mudu Sangha Samskaranalu-Aru Dalita Srenulu, Andhrajothy Sunday, August 13, 1995.

Dangle, Arjun (Ed.), Poisoned Bread, Bombay: Orient Longman, 1992.

Das, Bhagawan. "*Moments* in the History of Reservations," *The Economic and Political Weekly.* October 28, 2000.

Das, Bhagwan, "Moments in a History of Reservations", *Economic and Political Weekly*, October 28, 2000, pp. 3831-3834.

Dasgupta, S.N. "Dogmas of Indian Philosophy", Philosophical Essays, New Delhi: Motilal Banarsidas, 1982, pp. 208-233.

Daya Krishna, Political Development: A Critical Perspective, New Delhi: Oxford University Publications, 1979.

Daya Krishna, Social Philosophy-Past and Future, Shimla: Indian Institute of Advanced Studies, 1969.

Dayakrishna, "Three Myths about Indian Philosophy", Indian Philosophy: A Counter Perspective, New Delhi: Oxford University Press, 1991, pp. 3-15.

Delienge, The World of Untouchables Parias of Tamil Nadu, New Delhi: Oxford University Press, 1997.

Devasehayam, V. (ed.)., Frontiers of Dalit Theology, Delhi: ISPCK/Gurukul, 1997.

Dr. Anand Teltumbde, Ambedkar In and for the Post-Ambedkar Dalit Movement, Pune: Sugawa Prakashan, 1997.

Dr. B.R., Ambedkar Memorial Trust, B.R. Ambedkar Memorial Lectures, Hyderabad: Ambedkar Memorial Trust, 1993.

Dr. Javaraiah M V., Dr. Ambedkar, Father of the Constitution of India, Mysore: Siddharth Granthamala, 1992.

Drucker, HM., The Political Uses of Ideology, London: Macmillan, 1974.

Dumout, Louis, Homo Hierarchies: The Caste System and its Implications, Chicago: University of Chicago Press, 1974.

Freeman, Micheal, Edmund Burke and the Critique of Political Radicalism, Chicago: University of Chicago Press, 1980.

Gautam, C (Ed), Dr. Ambedkar Birth Centenary Souvenir, Vo1. I, United Kingdom: AICC, 1991.

Gautam, C (Ed), Dr. Ambedkar Birth Centenary Souvenir, Vo1. IV. United Kingdom; AICC, 1992.

Geeta. V, and Satish Deshpande, "Introduction: Career of Modernity", Journal of Arts and Ideas, Vol. 25-26.

Geetha. V. and S. V. Rajadurai, Towards a Non-Brahmin Millinnium: From Iyothee Thass to Periyar, Calcutta: Samya, 1998.

Gehlet, N.S., Indian Government and Politics, Jaipur: Rawat, 1996.

Ghosh, Sankar, Modern Indian Political Thought, Delhi: Allied Publishers, 1984.

Gokhale, Janyshree, From Concessions to Confrontation: The politics of an Indian Untouchable Community, Bombay: Popular Prakashan, 1993.

Gore, M.S., Social Context of an Ideology; Ambedkar's Political and Social Thought, New Delhi: Sage, 1993.

Gough, J.W., John Locke's Political Philosophy. Oxford: Clarendon Press, 1974.

Government of Andhra Pradesh, Justice Ramachandra Raju (Rtd.) Commission's Report on Schedule Castes in Andhra Pradesh.

Gowri Shankar, Juluri. (Ed.), Ventade Kalalu (Haunting Pens) Venukabadina Kulalu, Kodada: Spruha Sahiti, 2001.

Grover, Verinder (Ed.), Political thinkers of Modern India, No. 16, B.R., Ambedkar, New Delhi: Deep & Deep Publications, 1992.

Gunnel, John G., Political Theory: Tradition and Interpretation, Cambridge: Wintrop Pub. Inc, 1979.

Gupta, Dispankar (ed.), Social Stratification, Delhi: Oxford University Press, 1991.

Guru, Gopal. "Dr. Ambedkar's Concept of Political Power and the Question of Dalit Movement" In Dr. Ambedkar Memorial Lectures, Ambedkar Memorial Trust: Hyderabad, 1993.

Guru, Gopal, In Ghansham Shah (Ed.) "The Language of Dalit Bahujan Discourse", Dalit Identity and Politics, New Delhi: Sage, 2001.

Guru, Gopal, "Dalits: Reflections on the Search for Inclusion", Peter Ronald deSouza (Ed.), Contemporary India Transitions, New Delhi : Fundacao Orient and Sage Publications, 2000, pp. 59-72.

Guru, Gopal, "The Politics of Naming", Seminar 471, November 1998, pp. 14-18.

Guru, Gopal, Dalit Cultural Movement and Dialects of Dalit Politics in Maharashtra Mumbai: Vikas Adhyayana Kendra, 1997.

Guru, Gopal, "Dalit Movement in Mainstream Sociology", *Economic and Political Weekly*, April 3, 1993.

Guru, Gopal, Polilics of culture in Maharashtra, *Economic and Political Weekly*, October 8, 1994.

Guru. Gopal, "Understanding the Category" Dalit Vikalp VI/2.

Harrison, Selig. S., "Caste and Andhra Communities", The American and Political Science Review, Vol. 1, No. 2, pp. 378-401.

Hasan, Suroor, "It is Now a Caste Struggle", *The Hindu*, May 1, 1994.

Herida, Rudolf C., "Subaltern Alternatives on Caste, Class and Ethnicity", Contributions to Indian Sociology 34, 1, 2000, New Delhi: Sage, pp. 38-61.

Hoarse Quinntin (ed.), Antonio Gramsci, Selections from Political Writings, London.

Hoffman, John, Gramscian Challenge, Coercian and Consent in Marxist Political Theory, Oxford: Basil Blackwell, 1986.

Ilaiah, K., Why I am Not a Hindu, Calcutta: Samya, 1996.

Ilaiah, Kanche. "Ambedkar is Still Relevant", Andhra Pradesh Times, December 6, 1996.

Ilaiah, Kanche, "Caste and Contradictions", *Economic and Political Weekly*, Oct. 22, 1994.

Independence, Cambrdige: Cambrdige University Press, 1990.

Iyer, Raghavan (ed.), The moral and political writings of Mahathma Gandhi, Vol. 1 & 2, New Delhi : Oxford University Publications, 1986.

Janaiah. M., Dalit Politics in Andhra Pradesh: A Case Study of Bahujan Samaj Party, Jayal, Niraja Gopal (ed.), Democracy in India, New Delhi: Oxford University Press, 2001.

Jayashree P.M., Cynthias T, Ajai M., M.A. Britto and Aloysius Irudayam (Ed.) National Campaign on Dalit Human Rights Dalit Human Rights Violations; Atrocities against Dalits in India National Public Hearing April 18-19, 2000, Chennai Case Papers: Summary Jury's Observations and Recommendations.

Je. Sree. Potee Anadam Vidduram -Kutra Anadam Kruram, Andhrajyothy Sunday, February, 18, 1996.

Joint Action Committee (JAC), Negotiating Gender and Caste, *Economic and Political Weekly*, October, 28, 2000.

Juergensmayer, Mark, Religion as Social Vision; The Movement against Untouchability in 20th Century Punjab. Berkely: California University Press, 1982.

Kadam, K.N. (Comp.), Dr. Bahasahed Ambedkar and the Significance of His Movement: A chronology, Bombay: Popular Prakashan, 1991.

Kallekar K.K & A.S. Chansalkar, Political Ideas and Leadership of Dr. B.R., Ambedkar, Pune : Viswam Publications, 1989.

Kalyana Rao, G. Antarani Vasantham (Untouchable Spring), Hyderabad: Virasam, 2000.

Kamble, N.D., Deprived Castes and Their Struggle for Equality, New Delhi: Ashish Publication Rouse, 1983.

Kameshwara Rao, N.V & MVT Raju. "Malas and Madigas: Anthropological study of two Scheduled Castes of Telangana", Journal of Social Research, Vol. 8, 1979, pp. 59-68.

Kaannabiran, Kalpana. (Ed.) Sarihaddululeni Sandhyalu: Feminist Rajakeeyalu, Karyacharana Prasnalu, Hyderabad: Swecha Prachuranalu, 1995.

Karlekar, Hiranmay, The Mirror of Mandal. Social Justice, Caste, Class and Individual, Delhi: Ajanta, 1992.

Karunakaran, K.P., The Phenomenon of Nehru, New Delhi: Gitanjali Prakasan, 1979.

Kesava Kumar P., "Performance of Social Memory-In Search of Dalit Culture", presented in Conference of Dalit Intellectual Collective, Chennai, 23-25 of Feb, 2005.

Kesava Kumar, P., "Emergence of Dalit Novel in Telugu: An overview", Inukonda Thirumali (ed), South India: Regions, Cultures and Sagas, New Dellhi, Biblio Matrix, 2004. pp. 163-170.

Kesava Kumar. P., Jiddu Krishnamurti's Conception of Tradition and Revolution: A Critical Study, Ph.D. Dissertation submitted to University of Hyderabad, 1997.

Kesava Kumar & K. Satyanarayana (Eds.), Dalit Manifesto (An Anthology of Dalit Poems), Hyderabad: Vishphotana, 1995.

Kesava Kumar and K. Satyanarayana (Eds.), Dalit Manifesto, Hyderabad: Vishpotana, 1995.

Khabde, Dinkar, Dr. Ambedkar and Western Thinkers, Pune: Humans Printing Press, 1989.

Kheer, Danajay, Ambedkar Life and Mission, Bombay: Popular Prakasan, 1972.

Khilnani, Sunil, Idea of India. London: Penguin, 1998.

Knowles, Dudley, Political Philosophy London: Routledge, 2004.

Ko. Pra, Minority B. C. Kulalu:Samajika-Ardhika-Rajakeeya, Stitigathulu Hyderabad: Vikas Graphics, 2000.

Kohli, Atul (Ed.), The Success of India's Democracy, Cambridge: Cambridge University Press, 2001.

Kohli, Atul, Democracy and Discontent, Cambridge: Cambridge University Press, 1991.

Kothari, Rajni, "Rise of the Dalits and the Renewed Debate on Caste", Partha Chatterjee (Ed.), State and Politics in India, New Delhi: Oxford University Press, 1998, pp. 439-458.

Kothari, Rajni, "Essence of Mandal Report", *Mainstream*, Oct. 6, 1990.

Kshira Sagar, R.K., Dalit Movements in India, New Delhi: MD Publication, 1994.

Kuber W.N., B.R., Ambedkar, New Delhi: Publications Division, 1990.

Kymlicka, Will, Contemporary Political Philosophy : An Introduction, Oxford: Clarendon Press, 1990.

Lakshminarasaiah, G., The Essence of Dalit Poetry: A Socio-Philosophic Study of Telugu Dalit Poetry, Hyderabad: Dalitasana, 1999.

Laski, H J., The Rise of European Liberalism: An Essay in Interpretation, London: Unwin Books, 1971.

Laslett, Peter and WG Runcimen (eds.), Philosophy, Politics and Society, London: Lawrence and Wishart, 1978.

Laxman Rao, S., Society, State and Positive Discrimination: Institutional Interface with Mandal Commission, Ph.D dissertation submitted to University of Hyderabad, 1999 (un-published).

Laxmi Narasaiah, G. and Tripuraneni Sreenivas (Eds.), Chikkanavutunna Pata (Thickening Song), Vijayawada: Kavitvam, 1995.

Laxminarasaiah (Ed.), Padunekkinapata (An anthology of Dalit Poems) Vijayawada: Dalita Sane Prachrunalu, 1996.

Laxminarasaiah, G., Dalita sahityanikee Viplava Sahityanikee Drukpadhallo Tedavundi, *Andhrajyothy Sunday*, December 17, 1995.

Lerch, Jens., "Politics of the Poor: Agricultural Labourers and Political Transformations in Uttar Pradesh", *The Journal of Peasant Studies*, Special issue on Rural Labour Relations in India, Vol. 26, Number 2, 3 January-April, 1999.

Locke to Croce, London: Longman, 1978.

Lokhande, G. S., Bhima Rao Ramji Ambedkar, New Delhi: Sterling, 1977.

Lynch, Owen, Politics of Untouchability, New York: Columbia University Press, 1969.

M. Phil Dissertation Submitted to University of Hyderabad, 1999.

Mahajan, Gurpreet, Democracy, Difference and Social Justice, Delhi: Oxford University Press, 1998.

Mahajan, Gurupreet, "Ambedkar in Retrospect," *Economic and Political Weekly*, Jan. 25, 1994.

Mahar, Michael J., The Untouchables in Contemporary India, Jaipur: Rawat Publications, 1998.

Mallick, Ross, Indian Communism Opposites, Collaboration and Institutionalisation, Delhi: Oxford University Publications, 1994.

Manteiro, Anjali and Lakshmi Lingam., "Towards a common voice : An introduction to movements and campaigns in India", *Indian Journal of Social Work*, Vo1. 59, Issue 1, January, 1998, pp. 3-33.

Mendelsohn, Oliver and Upendra Baxi (ed.)., The Rights of Subordinated People. Delhi: Methenecon, 1987.

Michael, S. M. (Ed.), Dalits in Modern India: Vision and Values, New Delhi: Vistaar Publications, 1999.

Mitra, Subrata Kumar (Ed.), Politics of Positive Discrimination: Across National Perspectives, Bombay: Popular Prakasan, 1990.

Moffalt, Michael, The Untouchable Community in South Asia, Princeton: Princeton University Press, 1979.

Mohanty, Manoranjan, "Beyond the Mandal Commission", *Third Concept*, October, 1990.

Moon, Vasant, (Tr. Asha Damle), Dr. Babasaheb Ambedkar, New Delhi: National Book Trust, 2002.

Mujtebe Sayed Ali., "Agony of Mandalized Youth", *Mainstream*, Octobrer. 6, 1990.

Nagaraj D.R., The Flaming Feet : A Study of Dalit Movement in India, Bangalore: South Forum Press, 1993.

Narain A.K. and D.C. Ahir (Eds), Dr. Ambdekar, Buddhism and Social Change, Delhi: B. R., Publishing Corporation, 1994.

Narasimha Reddy, D. "Karamchedu: A dialectic without Development", *Economic and Political Weekly*, September 1985.

Nigam Aditya, Secularism, Modernity, Nation, Epistemology of the Dalit Critique, *Economic and Political Weekly*, November 25, 2000.

Oliver Mendelsohn and Marka Vicziany, The Untouchables: Subordination, Poverty and the State in Modern India, Cambridge: Cambridge University Press, 1998.

Omvedt, Gail., Dalits and Democratic Revolution : Dr. Ambedkar and Dalit Movement in Colonial India, New Delhi: Sage Publications, 1994.

Omvedt, Gail., "Kanshiram and the Bahujan Samaj Party" In K.L. Sharma (ed.), Caste and Class in India, New Delhi: Rawat Publications, 1998.

Omvedt, Gail., Dalit Visions, New Delhi: Orient Longman, 1995.

Omvedt, Gail., Liberty, Equality, Community, Dr. Babasaheb Ambedkar's vision of a New Social Order, 2000. In www. Ambedkar. org/Research.

Omvedt, Gail., Liberty, Equality, Community; Dr. Babasaheb Ambedkar's Vision of a New Social Order, Dr. Ambedkar Memorial Lecture, organised by Dr. Ambedkar Chair in Sociology, Jawaharlal Nehru University, New Delhi, 2004.

Omvedt, Gail., Reinventing Revolution: New Social Movements and the Socialist Tradition in India, New York: An East Gate Book, M.E Sharpe, 1993.

Omvedt, Gail., Reinventing Revolution: New Social Movements and the Socialist Tradition in India, New York: An East Gate Book, M.E. Sharpe, 1993.

Padma Rao, Katti, Caste and Alternative Culture, Madras: Gurukul Luthern, 1999.

Padma Rao, Katti, Dr. B.R., Ambedkar: The visionary, Ponnur: APDSP, 1994.

Pai, Sudha, Dalit Assertion and the Unfinished Democratic Revolution, The Bahujan Samaj Party in Uttar Pradesh, New Delhi: Sage, 2002.

Pai, Sudha, "Dalit Assertion in UP : Implications for Politics", *Economic and Political Weekly*, September 13, 1997.

Panikkar K N., "Towards a Hindu Nation", *Frontline*, February 12, 1999.

Pantham, Tomas and Kenneth L. Duetsch (Eds.), Political Thought in Modern India, New Delhi.

Patil, Sharad, "A New Way of Life : Towards a Synthesis of Marx and Ambedkar", *Mainstream*, January 24, 1995.

Plamentz, John, Democracy and Illusion, London: Longman, 1973.

Politics in India, Delhi: Oxford University Press, 1997.

Prakash, Nirupama, Schedule Castes (Socio-economic Changes), Allahabad : Change Publications, 1989.

Prakash, Prem, Ambedkar, Politics and Schedule Castes, New Delhi: Ashish Publishing House, 1993.

Prasad, Chandra Bhanu, Dalit Dairy: 1999-2003, Reflections on Apartheid in India, Chennai: Navayana, 2004.

Proceedings of National Seminar, Dr. B.R., Ambedkar Relevance of his Thoughts, 20th -21st February, 1999, Hyderabad Jubilee Hall, 1999.

Punnelekar, S.P., "Untouchability and Social Change", *Mainstream*, Republic Day Issue, 1983.

Pushpendra, "Dalit Assertion Through Electoral Politics", *Economic and Political Weekly*, Vol. 34, No. 36, 1999, pp. 2609-2618.

Quinton, Anthony, Political Philosophy, Oxford: Oxford University Press, 1977.

Raghavendra Rao, K., Babasaheb Ambedkar, New Delhi: Sahitya Academy, 1998.

Rajasekarayya, A.N., B.R., Ambedkar : The Quest for Social Justice, New Delhi: Uppal Publishing House, 1989.

Rajasekhar V.T and M. Gopinath., Text Book on Dalit Movement in India (Meaning and Message), Bangalore: Dalit Sahitya Academy, 1994.

Rajsekhar Shetty, V.T., Dalit Movement in Karnataka, Bangalore: Christian Institute for the Study of Religion and Society, 1978.

Ram, Nandu, "Dalit Movement in India: A Perspective from the Below", *The Indian Journal of Social Work*, Vol. 59, Issue 1, January 1998.

Ramana Reddy, K.V., Caste and Class in India (Seminar papers), Bombay: All India League for Revolutionary Culture, 1988.

Ramaswamy, Uma, "SC's in Andhra: Social Change", *Economic and Political Weekly*, IX, 29, July 20, 1974.

Ranganayakamma, Dalita Samasya Parishkaraniki Budhudu Chaladu! Ambedkaru Chaladu! Marx Kavali! (For Resolving the Dalit Problem, Neither Ambedkar nor Buddha are Solutions! A Marx is Required!). Hyderabad: Sweet Home Publications, 2000.

Rao, M.S.A. (Ed.), Social Movements in India, New Delhi: Manohar, 2002.

Ratnaiah, K., Social Change Among Malas, New Delhi: Discovery Publishing House, 1991.

Rawls, John, Political Liberalism, New York: Cambridge University Press, 1993.

Ray, A.K., "Anti Reservation Movement", *Economic and Political Weekly* August 10, 1985.

Rege, Sharmila, "A Dalit Feminist Standpoint of View", Seminar 471, November 1998, pp. 47-52.

Rodrigers, Velerian, Making a tradition critical in Labour and Meaning of Dalit Movement, Peter Robb (Ed.), Dalit Movements : The Meanings of Labour in India, Oxford: Oxford University Press, 1994.

Rodrigues, Valerian, The Essential Writings of B.R., Ambedkar, New Delhi: Oxford Press, 2002.

Sabine, George H., A History of Political Theory, New Delhi: Oxford and IBH Publishing Co., 1973.

Sakshi, Human Rights Watch, A. P. Dalit Human Rights Monitor-2000, Andhra Pradesh Hyderabad: Sakshi, July 2000.

Sangarakshita, Ambedkar and Buddhism, Glasgow: Windhouse Publications, 1986.

Sanjeevi, K., Nirdishatanundi Anirdhisthataku, In S. V. Satanarayana (Ed.), Dalitavad Vivadalu, Dalitavada Vivadalu, Hyderabad: Visalandhra Publishing House, 1999.

Sarkar, Sumit, "Indian Democracy: The Historical Inheritance. "In Atul Kohli (Ed.) The Success of India's Democracy, Cambridge: Cambridge University Press, 2001.

Satruguna M., "Andhra Pradesh: All Kapus as B. C's: Reducing reservation to a Farce", *Economic and Political Weekly*, September 10, 1994.

Satya Murthy T.V. (Ed.), Religion, Caste, Gender and Culture in Contemporary India, Delhi: Oxford University Press, 1996.

Satyanarayana, A., Dalit Identity and Consciousness in Colonial Andhra 1917-47, Vikalpa VI/2, 1998.

Satyanarayana, K., Eee potee venaka vunnadi Kutra, Andhrajothy Sunday, January 28, 1996.

Satyanarayana, K., "Yevari Vata Variki Dakkalsinde", *Andhrajyothy Daily*, January 2, 2005.

Satyanarayana, S.V., Dalitavada Vivadalu (Debates and Controversies on Dalitism), Hyderabad: Visalandhra, 1999.

Satyanarayana, S.V., Streevada Vivadalu (Debates and Controversies on Feminism), Hyderabad: Visalandhra, 1997.

Seneviratne, H.L. (Ed.), Forging of Caste and Community in India and Sri Lanka, New Delhi: Oxford University Press, 1997.

Seth, D. L., "Caste and Secularisation Process in India", Peter Ronald deSouza Contemporary India Transitions, New Delhi: Fundacao Orient and Sage Publications, 2000, pp. 237-263.

Shah, Ghanshym, State and Social Movements, New Delhi: Sage Publications, 2000.

Sharma, K.L. (Ed.), Caste and Class in India, Jaipur: Rawat Publishers, 1998.

Sharma, K.L. (Ed.), Social Inequality in India, Delhi: Ajanta, 1992.

Shonalkar, Vandana, "An Agenda for Gender Politics", *Economic and Political Weekly*, Januaury 2-5, 1999.

Shourie, Arun, Worshipping False Gods; Ambedkar, and the Facts which have been Erased, New Delhi: Harper Collins Publishers, 2000.

Shyamala, Gogu. (Ed.), Nallapoddu-Dalit Women Literature 1921-2002 (The Black Dawn), Hyderabad: Hyderabad Book Trust, 2003.

Sikhamani, Dalita Sahitya Tatvam (Dalit Literary Criticism), Hyderabad and Tenali: Literary Circle, 1998.

Skinner, Quentin, The Return of Grand theory in Human Sciences, Cambridge.

Srinivas M.N., Caste: Its Twentieth Century Avatar, Delhi: Penguin India, 1976.

Srinivas, M.N., Dominant Caste and other Essays, New Delhi: Oxford University Press, 1987.

Srinivasulu, K., "Andhra Pradesh: BSP and Caste Politics", *Economic and Political Weekly*, October 1, 1994.

Srivastva, S. P., "Dynamics of Dalit Oppression", *Eastern Anthropologist,* July-December 1997.

Sudhakar, Yendluri, Mallemoggala Godugu (The Umbrella of Jasmines) Madiga Kathalu, Hyderabad: Dandora, 1999.

Sundar Rajan, R., The Primacy of Political, Delhi: ICPR, Oxford University Press, 1991.

Sundararaju, Nagappagari, Chandala Chatimpu, Hyderabad: Madiga Sahitya Vedika, 1996.

Sundararaju, Nagappagari, Madigodu (Madiga's Life Stories), Hyderabad: Madiga Sahitya Vedika, 1997.

Tarakam, Bojja (ed), The First All India Dalit Writers Conference, (21-22 October 1987), Hyderabad: Dr. B.R., Ambedkar Memorial Trust, 1994.

Tarakam, Bojja, Kulam-Vargam Hyderabad: Hyderabad Book Trust, 1996.

Teltumbde, Anand 'Ambedkar': In and for the Post-Ambedkar Dalit Movement. Pune: Sugawa Prakashan, 1997.

Teltumbde, Anand, Ambedkar on Muslims Mumbai: VAK Publications, 2003.

Teltumbde, Anand, Anti-Imperialism and Annihilation of Castes, Dambivali: Ramai Prakashan, 2005.

The Bhopal Declaration (Document), Charting a New Course for Dalits for the 21st Century Bhopal Conference, Bhopal, India, 12-13, January 2002.

Thirumavalavan, (Tr. Meena Kanda Swamy), Talisman Extreme Emotions of Dalit Liberation, Calcutta: Samya, 2003.

Velaskar, Padma and G.C. Wankhede, "From old stigma to new: Exploring the Changing Identity of Urban Educated Dalits", *Indian Journal of Social Work*, Vol. LVII, No. 1, January, 1996.

Venkat Rao, Mallela Vargeekaranatho Dakkedi Vatti Vistare! *Andhrajyothy Telugu Dality*, December 12, 2004.

Venkateswarlu D., Harijan-Upper Caste Conflict, New Delhi: Discovery Publishing House, 1990.

Vikas Adhyan Kendra, A Special Issue on "Perspectives on Dalit question and the Future of Dalit Politics", Vikalp VI/2, 1998.

Vincent, Andrews, Theories of State, Oxford: Basil Blackwell, 1989.

Virasam Guntur Unit Pomphlet September, "Rajyadhikara Poratamlone Dalithula Samasyalu Parishkaram Avutayi", Republished in *Arunatara*, January, 1997.

Volga,Vasanta Kannabhiran and Kalpana Kannbhiran, "Yejamani Audhalatho Yejamani Soudhanni Kulagottagalama", In S.V. Satyanarayana, (Ed.) Dalitavada Vivadalu, Hyderabad : Visalandhra Publishing House, 1999.

Wilkinson, T.S. and MM Thomas (eds), Ambedkar and the Neo-Buddhist Movement, Madras: Christian Literature Society, 1972.

Wilson, K., Political Philosophy of Oppressed Indian, Hyderabad: Booklinks Corporation, 1983.

Yellaiah,Vemula, Kakka (Dalit Novel), Nalgonda: Gosangi, 2000.

Zelliot, Eleanor, From Untouchable to Dalit; Essays on the Ambedkar Movement, New Delhi: Manohar, 1992.

Zoya Hasan (ed)., The State, Political Process and Identity, Reflection in Modern India, Delhi: Sage, 1989.

Index